# MEMORIES
# OF MY
# MOTHER

My mother Diana Westmorland
drawn by Sargent

# MEMORIES
# OF MY
# MOTHER

## Julian Fane

HAMISH HAMILTON
*and*
ST GEORGE'S PRESS

First published in Great Britain 1987
by Hamish Hamilton Ltd and St George's Press
27 Wrights Lane, London w8 5tz

British Library Cataloguing in Publication Data
Fane, Julian
Memories of my mother.
1. Westmorland, Diana Fane, Countess of
2. Great Britain—Nobility—Biography
I. Title
941.082′092′4      ct788.w4/
ISBN 0-241-12120-5

Typeset by Rowland Phototypesetting Ltd,
Bury St Edmunds, Suffolk
Printed in Great Britain by
St Edmundsbury Press Ltd, Bury St Edmunds, Suffolk

# List of Illustrations

# RELEVANT GENEALOGY

IN the early 14th century Thomas, son of Sir Thomas Lyster de Derby, married Isabel de Bolton who was the heiress of an estate in the Ribble Valley, owned thenceforth by the Lister (Ribblesdale) family for six centuries.

Thomas Lister, 1751–1826, was created 1st Lord Ribblesdale in 1797 in consideration of his various services to the nation.

THE 6th Baron Neville of Raby was created the first Earl of Westmorland: he was born in 1364 and died in 1425. The seat of the Nevilles was Raby Castle at Staindrop in Durham.

The second son of the 1st Earl of Westmorland was created Lord Bergavenny (later Abergavenny).

The daughter of the 6th Lord Bergavenny, called Mary Neville, married Sir Thomas Fane in 1599.

Their son Francis Fane was ennobled in 1624. The titles of his ancestor on his mother's side, Baron Burghersh and Earl of Westmorland, had become extinct by this time: he chose to revive them. He was thus the first Earl of the second creation. He married Mary Mildmay, only daughter of Sir Anthony Mildmay and heiress of Apethorpe in Northamptonshire.

Two points of minor interest: Sir Francis Fane, grandson of the 1st (Fane) Earl, was amongst other things a dramatist and wrote a comedy called *Love in the Dark* and a tragedy called *The Sacrifice;* and the 10th Earl of Westmorland was Lord Lieutenant of Ireland 1790–1795.

[ vii ]

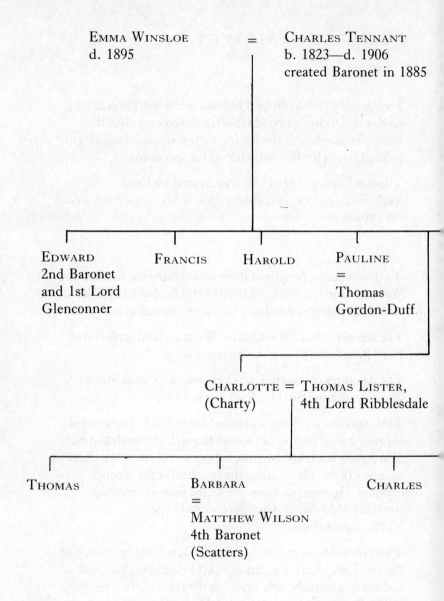

EMMA WINSLOE    =    CHARLES TENNANT
d. 1895                         b. 1823—d. 1906
                                   created Baronet in 1885

EDWARD          FRANCIS    HAROLD    PAULINE
2nd Baronet                                     =
and 1st Lord                                     Thomas
Glenconner                                      Gordon-Duff

CHARLOTTE = THOMAS LISTER,
(Charty)  |  4th Lord Ribblesdale

THOMAS          BARBARA          CHARLES
                         =
                MATTHEW WILSON
                4th Baronet
                (Scatters)

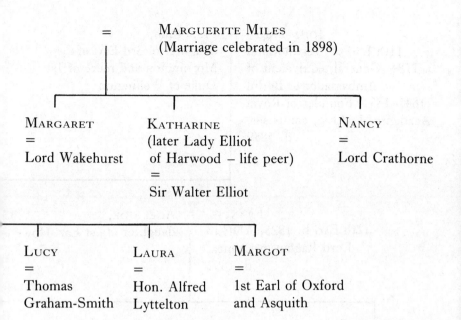

= MARGUERITE MILES
(Marriage celebrated in 1898)

MARGARET
=
Lord Wakehurst

KATHARINE
(later Lady Elliot
of Harwood – life peer)
=
Sir Walter Elliot

NANCY
=
Lord Crathorne

LUCY
=
Thomas
Graham-Smith

LAURA
=
Hon. Alfred
Lyttelton

MARGOT
=
1st Earl of Oxford
and Asquith

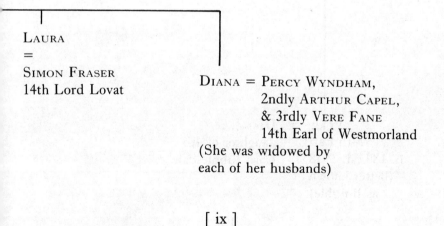

LAURA
=
SIMON FRASER
14th Lord Lovat

DIANA = PERCY WYNDHAM,
2ndly ARTHUR CAPEL,
& 3rdly VERE FANE
14th Earl of Westmorland
(She was widowed by
each of her husbands)

JOHN FANE, = PRISCILLA,
11th Earl of Westmorland    daughter of 3rd Earl of
b. 1784, General, equivalent of    Mornington and niece of 1st
Ambassador to Berlin    Duke of Wellington
1841–1851, Founder of Royal
Academy of Music, composer,
d. 1859

FRANCIS, = ADELAIDE,
12th Earl b. 1825, ADC to    daughter of 1st Earl Howe
Lord Raglan in Crimea,
d. 1891

ANTHONY, = SYBIL,
13th Earl    daughter of 4th
b. 1859,    Lord Rosslyn
Colonel, ADC
to H.M.,
d. 1922

VERE, = DIANA,
14th Earl    daughter of 4th
b. 1893 d. 1948    Lord Ribblesdale
(better known
as Burghie)

[ x ]

JULIAN = ADINE,
b. 1827, Diplomat, poet, | daughter of 6th Earl Cowper
translator of Heine, d. 1870

GRACE = 2nd Earl of
Londesborough

ETHEL = 1st Lord Desborough
(better known as Ettie)

HUGO,
3rd Earl of
Londesborough

JULIAN GRENFELL    BILLY GRENFELL

I SPENT ABOUT every third weekend with my mother at Lyegrove for the last twenty-five years of her life, at first as a bachelor, then with my wife.

This routine began as follows. She was probably feeling lonely. My father had been dead for a decade; and our old Nanny, who had become her friend, had recently expired in the erstwhile night-nursery. People came to see her and her garden in the summer. But the winters were solitary and long.

Moreover she needed reasons to stay on in the house she loved. It was too big and expensive. But so long as it remained a refuge for the family or any member thereof she could justify her refusal to move out.

Although she had five children – I was the fourth and in my late twenties at the time in question – the others seemed to be more preoccupied than I was. They were already married with offspring of their own, and houses and in-laws and so on, whereas I might be able and willing to get to and stay at our former home in Gloucestershire regularly. She never asked me to fill the empty space in her life. The relevant query was put to me by my sister June: 'Do you think you'll be going down to Lyegrove in future, when you're free and want to get out of London?' But I guessed she was speaking for Mama.

We did not know each other very well. Nanny had presided over my childhood. For the next nine years I was at boarding school; towards the end of the war I was called up and joined the army; and since then had been writing for all I was worth in rented rooms in the metropolis. Objectively speaking, and notwithstanding the same blood flowing in our veins, we were acquaintances on good terms.

And considering she had raised objections to my pursuit of a literary career, understandably enough although I was slow to understand them, I wondered whether she ever could or would sympathise with my work, a requirement of which was not to be saddled with distracting extraneous responsibilities such as those hinted at by June.

I therefore hesitated to reply positively, restrained by hearing the ominous note of the call of duty, and by scenting trouble.

Yet I wanted to help my mother. I was fond of her, and flattered by her enquiry via June and that she should think I could be helpful. And I must have inherited a small measure of her protectiveness. I admired her as person and parent; and because I would have hated to see or put her in the position of suppliant, I resolved rather in a rush to preserve her dignity at all costs.

Besides she was sixty-ish, verging on senility from the point of view of my relative youth, and I was reluctant to deny her anything in her last few years.

'Of course I'll be at Lyegrove whenever I can,' I told June. 'Do pass the message on to Mama.'

The significance of this brief exchange with my sister became increasingly clear as time wore on. I had given an explicit undertaking and entered into a sort of contract to support my mother. The practical problems of doing so until she died – still at Lyegrove – in 1983 in her ninety-first year were taxing. The penalty for not making my contribution to the efforts of the family to keep her well and happy would have been an unacceptably guilty conscience. The rewards were twofold: we drew closer together, and I am glad to remember it.

THERE WAS MORE to my mother than met the eye. I mean that although she considered her health was poor, or because she therefore took care of it, she lived to be ninety, and that in spite of a nervous sensibility her outstanding characteristic was courage.

Yet she seems to have been the cause of concern to everyone connected with her, and she inspired others to shield and cosset her, and seek her gratitude and praise.

I would say three factors were productive of the contra- diction between what I think she was and how I know she was treated.

The first was her beauty, and her look of beautiful fragility which was to some extent misleading.

And then her attitude of rueful melancholy or comical plaintiveness was apt to summon comforting compassion- ate laughter and reassurance. That attitude was a speciality of the family she was born into – a kind of jocular stoicism that recognised and mocked the machinations of fate. For example the word 'jolly' might well be substituted for the word 'tragic': 'Dear old X has been run over by a bus – jolly, isn't it?' Catastrophes often provoked giggles that were an antidote to gloom, expressive of a sense of helplessness and sparing of the embarrassment of a parade of emotion. Her ability to giggle was endearing and helped to keep her young. It startled those who were less appreciative of a joke than she was, or had not plumbed the sophisticated possibility of laughing in order not to cry. But perhaps they regarded it as weakness of intellect and another reason to be nice and kind to her.

Secondly she had been stricken by grief after grief until she was middle-aged. The catalogue of her bereavements seems too bad to be true. Throughout her childhood her mother was dying of TB. She was born in 1893 and lost one of her two brothers in 1904 – killed on active service in the army; her mother in 1911; her first husband after a few months of marriage in 1914; her other brother in 1915; her second husband – again after mere months of marriage – in a car crash in 1921; her father in 1925; one of her sisters in 1943 and her third husband – my father – in 1948 when she was fifty-five.

She bequeathed to me piles of letters to sort out – nearly all of condolence. Clearly the correspondents had to rack their brains for new words to say sorry with to the sweet inoffensive girl who was being turned into a sort of punch-bag for destiny to pummel. Typically a female friend wrote thus towards the end of the morbid saga of her youth: 'Oh my poor little darling, another crushing blow! I can't bear to think of all you've been through. I can't imagine how you have survived it. Yet because you have survived so far and so triumphantly I know you will go on surviving. What can I do? Believe me, I would do anything in the world to make you a tiny bit happier than you must be at present . . .'

My suggestion is that people continued to do things to make her happier because she retained an aura of having been sad, or, to put it another way, because, unassuming as she was, she had learned from sorrow to expect to be deferred to and indulged.

Thirdly she was aristocratic – and I venture to use the term despite my knowledge that in the context of our marvellously fluid social system it is as difficult to define as 'gentleman.' Her father, also her third and last husband, were titled; but peers and peeresses are not necessarily endowed with the superior qualities of the true aristocrat. Her father was the scion of a grand old family; but again a long pedigree is no guarantee of behaviour worthy of comparison with the ideal of aristocracy. And she was or had been rich; but impoverishment did not alter her bearing or conduct.

Certainly a gentle woman, refined, charitable, loth to upset anyone, she was nonetheless fearless in defence of her loved ones, principles and prejudices. Her self-assurance and native authority took precedence over her doubts and retiring disposition in the last resort. She lived to serve and paradoxically she was served. I suppose she possessed the quality called leadership, although her modesty, not to mention her opposition to feminism, would have scoffed at such a description.

LAURA LOVAT, HER sister and my aunt, carried the authoritative family trait a stage further – in her latter years, when I got to know her better and love her, almost to the point of imperiousness.

Aunt Laura's children, my Fraser first cousins, called it the divine right of Listers.

My mother was born Diana Lister, the youngest of the five children of Lord and Lady Ribblesdale of Gisburne Park in Yorkshire.

Much has been written about her father Thomas Lister, 4th Lord Ribblesdale, affectionately known as Tommy and Rib; also called The Ancestor on account of his patrician appearance and the old-fashioned and individualistic clothes he wore; also Le Grand Veneur, a reference to his fabled skills as horseman and huntsman and to his appointment as the last of the Masters of the Queen's Buckhounds, which hunted round Windsor; also in France, according to the writer Barbara Wilson who was his eldest daughter, Ce Grand Diable de Milord Anglais; and again The Governess's Hero, since at social gatherings he not only always would but was able to converse freely with the French governesses.

He is the subject of the famous portrait by John Sargent, which he presented to the nation in memory of his two sons Thomas and Charles: neither lived to inherit his title and transmit his name.

The Lister or Lyster family was going strong in the fourteenth century and probably earlier: not until 1300 were records kept in the West Riding of Yorkshire. The first Baron Ribblesdale was raised to the peerage in 1797 in consideration of his political and martial services. He was an M.P. for many years and organised regiments to defend the country from Napoleon, Lister's Light Dragoons, The Yorkshire West Riding Cavalry, and the unsuitably named Craven Legion – but I imagine and hope the word craven did not have a double meaning in his day. He planted trees without number, including 1,200,000 oaks in the Ribble Valley.

My mother's grandfather – her father's father – perished long before she was born. He was a spendthrift and gambler, and had to let Gisburne and take his wife and children to France, where life was cheaper. He managed to ruin the family all the same and finished by shooting himself.

His eldest son came into the title and not much else in 1876. But in 1877 he married Charlotte Tennant, one of the eight daughters and eleven children sired by Charles Tennant, created baronet in 1885, a Scottish industrialist and financier of genius, who seems to have paid the mortgages and debts his son-in-law was embarrassed by and enabled him to regain possession of his ancestral home and estate.

Sir Charles Tennant is said to have given each of his daughters a dowry of a quarter of a million pounds, probably the equivalent of between five and ten million in today's money. He owed some of his wealth to that essential element of genius of any kind – luck. For instance to oblige a friend on the verge of bankruptcy he agreed to buy all the shares he owned in some clapped-out gold mine, which cheap investment immediately began to yield an annual return of £250,000. Evidently he was an exception to the rule of Scottish stinginess, at any rate where his children were concerned. I understand that he footed the bill for the large family mansion the Ribblesdales built at 32 Green Street, Mayfair.

The Tennants of my grandmother Charty Ribblesdale's generation were Souls. She and her full sisters, whose married names were Pauline Gordon-Duff, Lucy Graham-Smith, Laura Lyttelton and Margot Asquith, could be called the very heart of the Souls, that unconventional, highbrow and alarming set of Edwardian kindred spirits.

Incidentally at the age of seventy-five Sir Charles Tennant, then a widower, remarried and produced three more daughters – making the total up to eight: they were much younger than my mother although her aunts.

I never heard my mother comment on the marriage of her parents, what it was like, whether it was happy, possibly because she seldom observed it in operation. Doctors prescribed the fashionable cures for Charty's disease that are now known to be bad for it: dry thin mountain air, salty ozone. She cut herself off from her family, no doubt because of the real risk of contagion, and was sent with nurses to coastal places and sanatoria in Switzerland. She died at Wimbledon, where she had lived in a hut in the garden of a rented house.

Her children were allowed to stand outside the hut and speak to her if and when she was feeling well enough.

[ 8 ]

My mother's memories of her mother always saddened her. Charty jotted down details of her illness and her hopes and fears in a book of prayers as she lay dying. The document is deeply harrowing, and I must admit I have never been able to bear to read it right through.

MY MOTHER REMEMBERED being taken to Queen Victoria's funeral by her father and how concerned he was for her safety in the crowd and how agitated he became. He hoisted her onto his shoulders: she was eight years old. As he was a conspicuously courageous man in the hunting field and elsewhere, his agitation on her account impressed and touched her.

Again she was struck by his enjoyment of simple pleasures: 'His favourite dinner was poached eggs on toast in front of the fire.'

He was a Privy Councillor, Lord in Waiting to Queen Victoria, Chief Liberal Whip in the House of Lords, Alderman of the London County Council, Justice of the Peace, Trustee of the National Gallery and National Portrait Gallery, Captain (retd) of the Rifle Brigade. Oddly enough the Mastership of the Queen's Buckhounds was a political appointment. It seems to have been a thankless task, since deer could not easily be hunted in the suburban environs of Windsor, Egham and Staines even in the 1890s, and the Master's other main duty was to disappoint some fifteen hundred people who had applied for admission to the Royal Enclosure at Ascot: he complained of receiving applications from three thousand five hundred and having room for two thousand. He had to ride up and down the Ascot race-course in front of the royal procession, wearing hunting tophat, breeches and boots, and a glamorous green riding-coat with the golden band of his office slanting across his chest: the leashes of hounds could be attached to the band.

According to an obscure contemporary publication called *Yorkshire Leaders*: 'A better judge of horse and hound [than Lord Ribblesdale] it would be difficult to find.' He kept and hunted his own pack of hounds at Gisburne. All the members of the family were keen on sports, blood and otherwise. My grandfather and my Uncle Charles were both enthusiastic big-game hunters in India. My mother hunted to hounds and coursed with what she called long dogs, one of which she bought from Julian Grenfell when he was courting her, though whether or not it was the subject of his wonderful poem *To a Black Greyhound* I cannot say: and later on she took my brother and myself out shooting.

My grandfather was a typical representative of blood-sportsmen and sportswomen in that he loved animals as well as loving to chase them. He used to sit in the window of Brooks's Club, watching and waiting to rush out and do physical battle with any driver of a vehicle who beat his horse or horses up the hill of St James's Street. And in old age my mother resolved the contradiction of her sporting youth by becoming a near-vegetarian.

The world's attitude to killing animals for sport underwent an enormous change in her lifetime – and may be changing again. Rider Haggard was a best-selling popular author and could assume that it was a quality of heroism to kill so-called game, witness *King Solomon's Mines* published in the 1880s. In recent years Animal Rights fanatics, socialists eager to exercise the privilege of rooting out privilege, and sentimental city-dwellers without experience of the countryside, have advanced the opposite view with more or less force. But abolition of game laws and the outlawing of all blood-sports, which even the carnivores amongst them advocate, would leave their furry and feathered friends at the mercy of poachers and other unregulated predators, as has been discovered in Africa – sport is now being asked to pay the price of conservation there.

After the death of my grandmother Charty Ribblesdale my grandfather sold their house in Green Street and moved into the old Cavendish Hotel, where he had a suite of rooms and was looked after by the famed cook, wag and Cockney eccentric Rosa Lewis. My mother for all her broad-mindedness never approved of the arrangement. She was embarrassed by his relations with Rosa – living under her roof, taking her to the theatre and so on – although she was sure they were platonic. She shied away from the idea that Charty's successor should be a hotel-keeper with a racy and dubious reputation.

But my grandfather seems to have fallen into a depression both before and after the loss of his second and last son and heir Charles in the 1914 war: as a result of it his nerves and maybe his judgment were not what they had been. Perhaps Rosa's charm was her ability to soothe his troubled and often irascible breast. After all she could cope with his fellow-resident at the Cavendish Sir William Eden – father of Anthony 1st Lord Avon – whose temper was notoriously filthy.

She was most put out when in 1920 my grandfather married Ava Astor, the widow of John Jacob Astor who went down with the Titanic, and removed into her house in Grosvenor Square. Rosa was sarcastic in her earthy style at the expense of the second Lady Ribblesdale, whose misfortune it was to have had the maiden name of Willing.


AS FOR MY mother, she was distressed both by the marriage and ever afterwards by her response to it.

'I remember Father took us all into Hyde Park and broke the news.'

Her sisters Barbara and Laura apparently shared her instant sense of outrage. They felt he was somehow desecrating the memory of their good long-suffering mother.

'We sat on a bench in the Park, the four of us. Poor Father! I'm afraid we weren't a bit nice to him.'

'What was Mrs Astor like?'

'Very smart, and I suppose she was good-looking. Some people said she was beautiful. But we thought she was hard.'

'Why did he marry her?'

'I've often wondered. He was in his late sixties at the

time. He might have loved her, or he could have been worried about money. If he was hoping not to be lonely, he chose quite the wrong companion.'

'Why?'

'Soon after they were married she returned to America – and she stayed there. I don't know what happened between them. But I think she was proud of him and wanted to show him off to her American friends, and he wouldn't go with her, he refused to be exhibited, and so they separated.'

The theory that my grandfather's second marriage caused him to sink into another and deeper depression does not hold water. Also in 1920 – the year he wed Ava – he travelled to India alone and happily, and thereafter he spent time at Lyegrove with my mother, who would have commented on and probably complained of any unwonted gloominess on his part.

Shimi Lovat in his autobiography *March Past* claims that his mother Laura was Lord Ribblesdale's favourite daughter. He may be right for all I know. Yet my grandfather could hardly have been sweeter to my mother when Percy Wyndham was killed in 1914; and to help her to get over the death of Arthur Capel in 1921, he joined her in renting Lyegrove near Badminton in Gloucestershire.

The lure of Lyegrove was not only that it was a ready-made retreat in which a well-to-do widow could mourn and recuperate in the care of her fond father. The place was an ideal hunting-box on a grand scale: they also took it in order to hunt with the Beaufort Hounds – the Duke of Beaufort's kennels were a couple of miles down the road at Badminton. Moreover it was fairly close to Easton

[ 13 ]

Grey, the charming house where Charty's sister Lucy Graham-Smith had lived and my grandfather and his young family had spent annual winter holidays greatly looked forward to and enjoyed.

My mother's Aunt Lucy was no longer living there. She had moved out of the area after the accident that was fatal both to her husband and her home. Mr Graham-Smith's end could be the subject of an anti-cautionary tale. He was terrified of fire and his fire-precautions included a nightly tour of the exterior of the house, paraffin lamp in hand. One evening he slipped in the hall, dropped the lamp which spilled paraffin and set it alight, and was burned to a cinder along with the building.

But my mother's memories of Easton Grey and that part of Gloucestershire seem to have been exclusively pleasant, and no doubt the same applied to her father's. I would guess that nostalgia was amongst the attractions of Lyegrove; also the softer climate of the south – Yorkshire's weather was too harsh for her and may have become so for him.

Their co-habitation worked rather well, or anyway to her satisfaction, otherwise she would not have wanted to buy Lyegrove later on.

Yet when she was old she would reproach herself for having neglected her father in his last illness.

'I don't even know what he died of. I didn't see enough of him. He was laid up in bed in Ava's house in Grosvenor Square. For some reason I never realised how ill he was. It was so stupid and unfeeling of me.'

She and Aunt Laura thought I had inherited a look of him. Once at Lyegrove when Aunt Laura was staying there – it was winter and dusk and misty – I was walking down the drive towards the front door as they prepared to close the shutters and draw the curtains. I was wearing a tweed cap and a borrowed tweed overcoat that was too big and reached below my knees.

They said to me: 'You gave us such a shock' – and explained why.

SOMEBODY UNDER THE pseudonym O wrote as follows in an obituary of Lord Ribblesdale: 'He was to his friends a definite and even a clear-cut personality, but, as a subject of portraiture, he is in many ways a baffling and elusive figure . . . The portrait by Sargent hardly exaggerates his individuality . . . To any conversation he imparted a flavour of his own, often with quaint and unexpected turns of speech, which made him one of the most delightful of companions.'

Tommy Lascelles, Charles Lister's contemporary and friend, who became the Right Honourable Sir Alan Lascelles with letters galore after his name, kindly took the trouble to type out for me those pages of his journal referring to my grandfather.

In 1910 Tommy writes: 'Ribblesdale dined, making a four with Charles [Lister], Timmy [Jekyll] and me. He was quite monumental, and kept us enthralled for three hours. I've never met anyone of that generation who can step down into ours like he can – which is remarkable, seeing that outwardly he's the most old-school of them all.'

Tommy's next entry is strange. Charty Ribblesdale died on 2 May 1911, yet on 27 May he writes: 'To Wimbledon. Ribblesdale and Barbara [Wilson] in astounding form, and I laughed myself sick. She is the most brilliant talker, and a jolly woman, though she tears people to pieces like a tigress.'

In September 1911 he visited Gisburne: 'The house is very Yorkshire – square, grey and Adam. There is a round dining-room, which is admirable . . . but has such an echo that diners think one another deafer than haddocks . . . We all went out for an organised lark on sundry horses. Barbara and Diana rode as one would expect R's daughters to, and look like Valkyries.'

The previous year my grandfather had broken a leg in four places hunting in Gloucestershire, and was still on crutches.

Tommy writes: 'There was a sad scene at luncheon when Rib became enraged with his three lovely daughters and shook his crutch at them, crying, "Blast the girls – the lamer one is the less they do for one!" – a most unjust accusation.'

In 1920 my grandfather travelled out to India – as stated – where he had done some soldiering in his youth and Tommy Lascelles was now ADC to the Governor of Bombay. Apparently he spoke of the new Lady Ribblesdale by whom he was not accompanied as 've beautiful Mrs Astor': did he really lisp in that way? 'However,' Tommy continues, 'he seems to have consoled himself by contracting an incredible number of intimate and wholly undesirable friendships on board his liner. When I drive him through Bombay, the car is halted every five minutes so that he can greet some flamboyant female with a Georgian salute and a cry of "ve top of the ve morning to you, Mrs X." He is a pronounced success here with old and young, for he keeps his almost unique power of shedding his years to suit his company . . . And he is still the prince of table-talkers.'

Tommy's final reminiscence, not part of his journal, dates back to 1916, when he was with his regiment on the Somme. 'One day I got a letter from Rib, saying that he and Mrs Warre Cornish were jointly preparing a memorial volume about Charles Lister, and would I send him any letters I might have. This request flummoxed me. As a matter of fact I had kept every line Charles had written me over the period of our friendship; but his epistolary style was frankly Rabelaisian and his matter intensely critical of his acquaintance. For no consideration would I allow anybody else to read his letters, let alone publish them. So after much cogitation I replied to Rib that all C's letters were locked up in a box in my Dorset home, and would he mind waiting until I was on leave and could let him have them. To this he agreed. When I got home a month or two later I spent hours copying out the bowdlerised version of the correspondence, which Rib and Mrs Cornish eventually used in their splendid book.'

My grandfather and Mrs Cornish, the superannuated wife of the Vice-Provost of Eton College, were not altogether successful at censoring letters from Charles to other people. Although they had let it be known that they would publish nothing hurtful of anyone's feelings, they included in the final text the following sentence: 'Mrs Benson is coming out [to India] to see [her son] Rex, which is a pity.'

The Prefatory Note to the book ends thus: 'Charles always dated his letters . . . mindful of Dr Johnson's dictum that Chronology is the eye of History.' Unfortunately my grandfather himself was not mindful of it. He seldom added the year or indeed the month to the day of the week on which he put pen or pencil to his doubled sheets of grey-green writing paper with hairs showing through. The absence of dates makes it difficult to arrange his letters in any comprehensible order, while the illegibility of his high-class scrawl presents another problem.

Most of his correspondence with my mother seems to be about plans. But felicitous phrases are reminders that he was the accomplished author of *The Queen's Hounds* and *Impressions and Memories*; and the passage below about Barbara, quirky, objective to the point of disloyalty, ironical, is representative at once of his sense of humour and that which he passed on to his descendants: 'Lady Wilson is at last better, and now looks less like nothing on earth. In spite of her indisposition her spirit is not quenched. She is now fighting with 1) her Parish Council, 2) the Rural District Council, and 3) the Duke of Devonshire – over their responsibilities for the repair of a few yards of road. She has notified the Duke that he must walk over her dead body before she will yield. Whether or not the nobleman will do so has not yet transpired.'

MY MOTHER CAN scarcely have known her brother Thomas, for he was fifteen years older than she was, joined the army when she was four, fought throughout the Boer War in South Africa, and was killed in a small colonial skirmish in Somaliland when she was eleven.

For Lord Ribblesdale, the knife must have been turned in the wound of the loss of his elder son by the information that he was chosen for the fatal mission because of being the best rider in the regiment: he had been taught by his father at Gisburne.

Pictures and photographs of Tommy Lister show a man with crinkly brown hair cut short, regular features and an earnest and dutiful expression. He was very brave. He was twice mentioned in despatches, won the D.S.O., and was recommended for the V.C.

I am proud of the courage of many of my relations. Reflected glory of the gallant kind is better than none, especially for somebody descended as I am from the gentleman in Shakespeare's Henry V who urges the King not to fight at Agincourt.

The Listers shrugged off wounds before penicillin was invented, although bullets and shrapnel caused blood-poisoning and gangrene, which were often lethal. Tommy was wounded at least once, and Lord Ribblesdale, having gone to South Africa to see him and ridden into range of the Boers armed with his umbrella, was shot in the posterior, much to his own and the family's amusement. And Charles was wounded repeatedly.

And Barbara married a D.S.O., and Laura was the wife, mother and aunt of D.S.O.s.

I was sixteen when Aunt Barbara died in 1943. My one clear memory of her is in Aunt Laura's flat in Hyde Park Mansions, off Edgware Road. She sat on a window-seat, smoking cigarettes called Cooltipt. She must have been ill, perhaps dying: she had black shadows under her heavy-lidded eyes and a greyish complexion. Her hair was wiry and iron-grey and her nose beaky, but even my purblind youth noticed the refinement of her countenance. She was extremely thin with bony graceful hands – more a wraith than a Valkyrie.

She was her brother Tommy's contemporary and, according to my mother, so fond of him that when he was killed she turned to and fell in love with his friend and brother-officer Matthew Wilson, later Sir Matthew Wilson Bart., more widely known as Scatters Wilson.

They were such an ill-assorted pair: she was literary, a blue-stocking, almost a scholar, and he a professional soldier, then a squire in the country and clubman in London, and incorrigible womaniser and gambler. Scatters' home was Eshton Hall in Yorkshire, only fifteen miles from Gisburne. I imagine he came over to commiserate with Barbara and consoled her as best he could. They were married in the year following Tommy's death – 1905.

Her husband was acknowledged to be funny and fun, to have a way with him, and the power to make people feel all the better for seeing him. But Tommy Lascelles writes of another visit to Gisburne: 'Scatters Wilson at poker took large sums of money off the three young men staying in the house, Edward Horner, Patrick Shaw-Stewart and me – and was given hell by Barbara for doing so.'

And my mother was none too kindly disposed towards Scatters, whose rakish proclivities cannot have done her sister much good.

'In London he left her alone evening after evening. He was out all day, and would come home for dinner and then leave as he was swallowing his last mouthful of coffee. He specialised in terms of endearment: he'd call her his darling and duck and pet and precious and heart's delight and lovey-dovey, and say there were friends waiting for him at the club to make a four for bridge. I believe he earned several thousand pounds every year playing cards. But he never stopped playing other games as well.'

They produced three children, Martin, the present baronet, and Tony and Peter who are now dead. Peter was the Chairman of Sotheby's for many years.

Aunt Barbara in the solitude of her marriage wrote *Dear Youth, The House of Memories* and *Relight the Lamp*. Her books were successful, especially *Dear Youth*, which, as its title suggests, tenderly and nostalgically describes her pre-marital past. They also testify to her deep love of France, its language and literature. As a girl she had studied and must have been happy there.

CHARLES LISTER WAS six years older than my mother and loved her dearly, as she loved him. He gave her a pretty black and white enamel box with a cracked lid, which she treasured and left to me. He wrote her many long letters, including his last one from the hospital ship *Gascon* moored off the Dardanelles.

In later life she did not often speak of him. If she should happen to see children playing with sticks she might warn: 'Once my brother Charles whirled round with a stick in his hand and hit me in the face. He was so terribly upset.' I recall brief mention of the facts that he had been tremendously clever and a fine character, or somebody's friend, or had temporarily veered from the liberal politics of the family towards socialism and organised a socialist gala in the park at Gisburne. She would explain that Sargent had drawn Charles with the sketched figure of a forbear in the background, because he had been struck by the likeness between them. But she said no more to me. Remembering him was probably always painful.

Her estimate of his virtues seems to have been an understatement. Friends and representatives of his generation who survived have included him amongst the leaders we lost in the Great War.

My mother was not wrong in respect of his brains. He won a Scholarship to Eton and an Exhibition to Balliol, and then got a First in Greats. He started a magazine at Eton, *The Outsider*, and a club at Oxford, The Orthodox Club, also a Committee for Lectures on Social Subjects. He organised a protest at Eton, and had it printed, signed by all prominent boys, and presented to the Headmaster by the trembling Captain of the School. According to Ronald Knox, legendary intellectual and wit and eventually Catholic priest and translator of the Bible, he was only just dissuaded from writing a letter of reproof to an Eton master which began: 'Sir, This kind of thing will not do . . .' All accounts of him agree that he was inspired by a passion for justice and to help the poor and weak. When he was sent down from Oxford as punishment for some tipsy misdemeanour, he went and worked at the Trinity Mission in the East End of London. Again Ronald Knox: 'He was a Socialist . . . before Labour became a fashion, petted by Society and patted gingerly on the back by dignitaries of the Church.' While he was a member of the Oxford branch of the Fabian Society its membership increased five-fold. He formed strong ties with the Oxford Trades Council and played a strong supporting role in a strike of girls employed by the Clarendon Press. An unnamed contributor to his father's memoir – *Charles Lister, Letters and Recollections* – sums up his three undergraduate years thus: 'He displayed . . . a steady working enthusiasm, a power of getting on with everybody and making everybody work, and a great gift of knowing what was practical and what was not.' His Oxford tutor writes of Charles in the year of his Finals: 'I never saw a man work so hard and so sensibly.'

At the same time he was neither a swot, nor exclusively political, nor a dull dog: dull dogs do not get elected to Pop at Eton. Coming from Ronald Knox, who knew what he was talking about, the following statement is extremely complimentary: 'His gaiety was infectious.' Those who were with him at school, university and afterwards, and in the army, harp on his humour.

Ronald Knox writes that when Charles entered the Diplomatic Service he did not abandon radical politics, he abandoned politics. But Lord Ribblesdale states that Charles changed his mind and came to disapprove of the methods of his former 'comrades.' He quotes from a letter from Charles to Tommy Lascelles: 'I feel the Labour grievance as strongly as ever, but I've lost faith in most of the remedies . . . If only they would get back to the old sober Trade Unionism . . . But a change of spirit in most of the Trade Unions is required.'

Another excerpt from another letter to another friend, Bruce Ottley, suggests his interests were simply widened by his diplomatic experience: 'I am thrilled by Weltpolitik.'

He took up his first post at the Rome Embassy in 1911, moved briefly to Constantinople [Istanbul], and volunteered for military service in 1914. Sir Rennell Rodd, his Ambassador in Rome, writes of Charles: 'The fine open face, the kindly voice, the unflinching honest eyes and the warm-hearted humorous smile made them [children] at home with him at once.' And: 'Of all the sorrows and infamies which those who are responsible for these disastrous years have brought upon us, few have touched me personally with such bitterness of resentment as the loss of this most gallant soul and honourable gentleman.'

He went out to the Dardanelles, was soon wounded and, while recuperating, invited to join the Foreign Office staff in London. He explained his refusal to Bruce Ottley: 'I feel I ought to see this thing through, and can't bear to think of leaving the wonderful fellows of my battalion.'

A brother-officer, Mr Heald, describes his return to active service thus: 'I think we began to shape ourselves the day that Lister – his wounds hardly healed – returned joyously to that sun-baked camp with its twin plagues of flies and dysentery, and declared that everything was very jolly and this sort of picnic was one of life's richest slices.' He goes on: 'There was no mess in the Peninsula so merry as ours, with Lister always on the most uncomfortable packing-case, declaiming and denouncing with that dear old stiff gesture of his which we came to know so well.' And finally: 'But the strongest impression I have of Lister was his eager sense of duty. Throughout the war I never met a man in whose heart there burned so steadily that first fine flame that sent us all out soldiering . . . He was ever on the look-out for something useful to be doing. His willingness to sacrifice himself seemed part of some high secret religion of his own; and those who mourn for him must realise that this, coupled with his serene disdain of danger, inevitably meant his fall sooner or later in the campaign.'

His commanding officer Sir Ian Hamilton wrote of him in a so-called Honours Despatch: 'For brilliant deeds of gallantry throughout our operations . . . He personally reconnoitred a Turkish communications trench, and, although wounded (for the second time), he . . . led forward a party to the attack. Subsequently he was a third time wounded and has since died . . .'

MY UNCLE CHARLES seems to have had no idea that third wound might be mortal. In his last letter he tells my mother: 'Don't write till I wire my permanent address,' and again in wording even more sinister in retrospect: 'I will wire Father as soon as I get to our final destination.'

He goes on: 'My darling, Excuse this scribble written in a pleasant state of coma, which cramps the style . . . You will have heard by now of my being wounded once more . . . The day had passed peacefully enough. But at about one o'clock the French began to [word indecipherable] and the Turks to retaliate rather effectively . . . So I thought I had better see what was going forward as my men had not been under shellfire before. I went down and found very little mischief had been done . . . and believed the ball was over. The Turks however had an unfortunate afterthought and plugged in a shell just behind me, damaging pelvis and bladder and both calves, but not seriously. I was operated on directly I got on board this ship: my poor old tummy is as full of tubes as a whistler's neck.'

By whistler he meant one of those horses with tubes

fixed in their necks to assist them to breathe: they whistle when they exert themselves.

He ends: 'We are at present circling these islands . . . I don't mind the Cook's Touring because it means I stick to the same doctor, and as matters stand I couldn't do much walking about. It has gone much cooler nowadays on Gallipoli – and many "wise virgins" are getting winter kits, but I can't believe we'll be such fools as to submit to the indignity of a winter campaign. Your C.'

Uncle Charles was eleven years old when drawn by Sargent in 1899. The beautiful mask of his boyhood developed into an adult countenance with large manly features, broad brow, heavy Roman type of nose and eyes that could be called smouldering, at least in repose.

What would he have wanted to do if he had lived?

Long ago I was asked out to dinner by Tommy Lascelles and Sir Lawrence Jones who wrote his series of autobiographical books – *A Victorian Childhood, An Edwardian Youth* etc – under the name L. E. Jones, and was known to his cronies as Jonah. Their intentions were to tell me all about their friend and my uncle, perhaps plumb my depths or shallows, and generously feed me. As opportunity offered, each of my hosts in turn drew me aside to suggest the other had not really belonged to Charles Lister's circle of intimates. Notwithstanding this disagreement they were agreed that Charles could have wanted to be Viceroy of India.

I found this answer a trifle disappointing. India had been independent for some time, and I was ignorant of the historical scope and power of its former rulers. I suppose I had hoped to hear that Uncle Charles aspired to one of the ideals – heroically literary, for instance, or political in the aristocratic Disraelian sense – which my raw romanticism would have considered fitting.

But Tommy Lascelles and Jonah Jones were realistic old gentlemen – they might have owed their existence as well as their eminence to their realism. They were trying to tell me that as Viceroy he could have indulged his passion to help the poor and weak to his heart's content, drawn on his diplomatic experience, utilised his practical common sense, and followed and even influenced the course of Weltpolitik – and his confidence in the divine right of Listers would have come in handy. Again they knew better than me that the vice-regal job had been extraordinarily difficult to do, let alone do well, and in suggesting he was equal to it they were paying him high tribute. And no doubt in their eyes it was more romantic than in mine. If they seemed to err on the side of dour and worldly caution, it was probably because of their membership of the generation that largely died of its romantic attitudes.

AN AMAZING AMOUNT of pretentious rubbish was written about the First World War, especially its earlier years, by combatants as well as non-combatants.

I am sorry to say my grandfather wrote thus of Charles joining the army: 'The Call had come upon him as the

Holy Ghost came down upon the Apostles – as a sudden great sound in the likeness of fiery tongues.'

The symbolism of fire and flame was overworked: Mr Heald wrote of the flame that burned in Charles' heart and had brought 'us all out soldiering.' I cannot believe all the soldiers burned altruistically to fight and perhaps die.

Charles himself expressed some peculiar views, for example when Rupert Brooke died of blood-poisoning at the age of twenty-seven: 'Rupert's was certainly a perfect death, and a very fitting close to a fine life.' And he wrote of Julian Grenfell's death from wounds to his mother Lady Desborough: 'He felt keenly, I am sure, that he was doing something worthwhile, the thing most worthwhile in the world . . . Surely the Lady he sought with tireless faith, the Lady for whom he did and dared so much on lonely paths, will now reward him?'

Many reasons have been advanced for the popular enthusiasm for that vile war: the upper class was expiating the guilt of feeling it was too rich, the middle class was relieving the boredom of its monotonous security, the lower class in its wretchedness and frustration was only too happy to lash out at somebody, and so on. The most interesting explanation I have come across was offered by Charles without any fancy trimmings to Ronald Knox: 'This war is primarily a search after the new.'

A poetic phrase, again in his letter to Lady Desborough, stands out from the generally matter-of-fact run of his correspondence: 'Julian had so many friends who felt for him as they felt for no one else, and a fierce light still beats at the scene of his passing . . .' Whatever the latter phrase may mean, it excites and impresses in the manner of William Blake.

But Charles was not a true poet and vocational writer like Julian Grenfell, the most original of those conscripts to literature who fought in the war: his originality may help to account for the feelings of Charles and so many others when he was killed.

Nowadays the poets of that war who bewailed man's inhumanity and the tragic wastefulness of bloodshed are more fashionable: they feed the fears and appeal to the self-pity of the present age. Julian wrote of the war: 'I never felt so well, or so happy, or enjoyed anything so much. It just suits my stolid health and stolid nerves and barbaric disposition. The fighting-excitement vitalises everything, every sight and word and action.'

He puts forward the best apology for war and for that matter blood-sport, and as it were thumbs his nose at priggish pacifists and humanitarians: 'One loves one's fellow-man so much more when one is bent on killing him.'

He also thought war 'horrible' and 'beastly', and might have written about it differently if he had had to endure the three years from 1915 to 1918, for of course the nerves of the author of *Into Battle* were not so stolid as he liked to think. Yet such an hypothesis does not invalidate the philosophy of the first stanza of his poem:

> The naked earth is warm with spring,
>     And with green grass and bursting trees
> Leans to the sun's gaze glorying,
>     And quivers in the sunny breeze;

And life is Colour and Warmth and Light,
    And a striving evermore for these;
And he is dead who will not fight;
    And who dies fighting has increase.


Julian Grenfell was that exceptional combination of man of action and literary genius, as brave in print as on the field of battle (he won the D.S.O.) or in the boxing-ring or on his death-bed in the hospital at Boulogne, debunker of the current political, religious, patriotic and maudlin humbug in respect of the war, artistically a traditionalist who scorned the second-hand, an aristocrat in social, artistic and existential terms – and as someone remarked the gentlest as well as the gallantest.

Patrick Shaw-Stewart, Fellow of All Souls and a Managing Director of Baring's Bank at the age of twenty-five, undoubtedly admitted to the innermost circle of Charles and Diana Lister's friends, scribbled a lesser-known poem about going into battle in his copy of *A Shropshire Lad*:


I saw a man this morning
    Who did not want to die;
I ask and cannot answer
    If otherwise wish I.

Fair broke the day this morning
    Against the Dardanelles;
A breeze blew soft, the morn's cheeks
    Were cold as cold sea shells.

[ 31 ]

But other shells are waiting
    Across the Aegean sea,
Shrapnel and high explosive
    Shells and hells for me.

O hell of ships and cities
    Hell of men like me.
Fatal second Helen,
    Why must I follow thee?

Achilles came to Troyland
    And I to Chersonese;
He turned from wrath to battle,
    And I from three days' peace.

Was it so hard, Achilles,
    So very hard to die?
Thou knowest and I know not –
    So much the happier I.

I will go back this morning
    From Imbros over the sea;
Stand in the trench, Achilles,
    Flame-capped, and shout for me.

Patrick Shaw-Stewart's poem was found after his death. He had received answers to his questions, the passionate dread and regret of which are still agonising. Julian Grenfell's achievement was to rise above the agony and, in the last lines of *Into Battle*, encourage and reassure the fighting man with the promise that

Day shall clasp him with strong hands,
And night shall fold him in soft wings.

I HAVE CHANGED my mind about Julian Grenfell for the last time.

When young I accepted without question that he was the nonpareil of chivalry, unrivalled hero, poet, athlete, the nation's irreplaceable champion, the first name on the list of fabled comrades and casualties of the 1914 war – his younger brother Billy, Raymond Asquith, John Manners, Patrick Shaw-Stewart, Edward Horner, not to mention my Uncle Charles – which reminded me of the roll-call of the fallen in Henry V; and he was anyway beyond reproach on account of having been my mother's great friend and flirt, if not suitor.

Later I reacted against his pugilist's face in some photographs; stories of him cracking his stock-whip in the Quad at Balliol and terrorising lesser mortals; and the blueness of his blood, and health, wealth and strength, both mental and physical strength – the altogether excessive range of blessings showered on him; and the incense offered up to his memory fifty years after his death by people like my poor Mama, who had probably been misled by calf-love. As for the list he had seemed to head, my iconoclasm compared it with Uncle Tom Cobbleigh and all.

[ 33 ]

Yet now I have come round to thinking he must have been at least as outstanding as his friends believed – he and to a lesser extent Billy Grenfell, sometimes called the Dioscuri, otherwise known as Castor and Pollux, sons of Zeus, horsemen and boxers and warriors of divine repute, translated into the starry firmament as Gemini, The Twins, and referred to by the poet Horace as clear-shining stars.

A pencil sketch of Julian by an unknown artist that belonged to my mother shows a finely shaped head and a countenance convincingly tough, yet with a benevolent and even tender expression.

And a last excerpt from a letter from Charles Lister to Ronald Knox sheds light on Julian's arrogance – often complained of – and again on his originality: 'They [the governing caste of undergraduates of Balliol] have neither Julian to suppress the plebs nor a good fellow like me to keep them in a good temper. Things worked very well [in the Balliol democracy] when I was there to cover up Julian's tracks, and Julian was there to make fresh ones . . . and overawe the rebellious . . . And envy cannot overlook the fact that he was a first-class writer of prose as well as poetry.'

Billy was his academic and possibly athletic superior. He won scolarships to Eton and Balliol, First Class Honours and every available prize, and Blues for boxing and tennis: he would have had a third Blue for running if he had not fallen ill at the wrong time. Both brothers were terrific boxers by professional standards, Julian of the fighter type, Billy a heavyweight said to smile seraphically as he knocked out opponents.

[ 34 ]

My mother had two letters from Billy amongst her papers. The first was written from his home at Taplow, Bucks, to hers at Gisburne, Yorks, evidently while she was still unattached. The date is New Year's Day.

'My darling, How is life in the bleak North? It goes well here, in what is known as the Monaco of England . . . Casie [his sister Monica] has now burst upon an astonished world. She was sick five times on Xmas Eve, but the brave girl was sufficiently recovered to entertain all the local Grimeses to a buffy dinner on Boxing Day . . . Write to me, my love, and tell me about life and death . . . It is a sobering thought that before the end of the year you are likely to be staggering towards the altar. Who will it be? May I hope? I am tired of giving wedding ps.'

The second letter congratulates her on her engagement to Percy Wyndham: 'My excuse for not having written to you before is my rage at the last of the Miss Listers having escaped me in the rush to the altar. The only chance now is to wait for Barbag's divorce, which cannot be long deferred. However, apart from green-eyed jealousy, I must admit you have chosen remarkably well. Let us also hope that Percy is immensely rich, and will repay our wedding gifts a thousand fold.'

Barbag may have been a nickname in general use for my Aunt Barbara, or else that ending was tacked on to words as a joke in the Grenfell private lingo. Three adjectives in the vocabulary invented by the Grenfells and Asquiths were: pointful, meaning having a point and being worthy of interest; Brahms, deriving from the composer and meaning delightful and soothing; and

Heygate, which was the name of an Eton master, meaning pompous and dull.

In parentheses: Geoffrey Madan attributes an entry about pomposity in one of his *Livres sans Nom* to M. Heyguet, a French variation on the name of the unfortunate Heygate. And of all private lingos Maurice Baring's seems strangest: he would add -umble to the first letters of words – thus, for example, he became Mumble Bumble, and the younger Lister sisters Lumble and Dumble.

My mother had also kept two of Julian's letters. Again one congratulates her on her engagement, but somewhat tensely: 'What luck for Percy! You ought to be a happy girl, too, because he is one of the best men in the world . . . I hear that you have been going the living best in Leics and cutting them all down [a reference to her performance out hunting] . . . Bless you, darling D, and the sum total of happiness to you. Don't write to me.'

The other is written from France during the war and surely after she was widowed: 'I brought three good long dogs back here with me, and we walk over deep sodden ploughed fields: but the French hares are not up to their class. I wonder if we shall ever hunt or course at Gisburne together? What fun we used to have! Shall I ever sell you another £5 dog? Write to me, darling, and *please* see me soon. J.'

I believe I was given my Christian name partly in honour of Julian Grenfell, and partly for the same reason he was given his, because my great-great-great-uncle and his grandfather was Julian Fane.

But the connection between my Lister mother and the Fanes is another story.

LAURA AND DIANA Lister as little girls were called The Dolls. They had pet names for each other, too, no doubt based upon the sad feeling that they were motherless, since Charty was ill and absent for so much of the time: Laura was Diana's 'Own Mummy' and Diana was Laura's 'Own Baby.' Even as married women with children they continued in letters to use the initials OM and OB.

Although they seem to have been similarly doll-like in their pretty infancy, they grew up to be more than pretty in different styles. Laura was very tall and long-limbed and graceful – Cynthia Asquith wrote of her 'lovely liquid movements'; and Diana smaller, neater, with more regular features in a narrower face, meriting the epithet often applied to her – dainty. As many books of memoirs attest they were much admired, one putting the other in the shade in the eyes of various interested parties.

In 1910 Laura married straight out of the schoolroom, that is to say when she was very young – eighteen or so.. Her husband Simon Lovat, Lord Lovat, was a grand gentleman of ancient Scottish lineage some twenty years older than she was. He was hereditary chieftain of the Clan Fraser; had raised his own regiment of Lovat Scouts to fight in the Boer War, just as his son and his nephew were to raise regiments in their day, respectively the Commandos and the SAS; had already won the D.S.O.

and the C.B., and was later to be K.T., G.C.V.O. and K.C.M.G.

The accounts in newspapers of their nuptials in London, the reception at 10 Downing Street lent by the bride's aunt Margot Asquith and the Prime Minister, the lists of guests and wedding presents, and reports of the loyal addresses and celebrations of clansmen and tenantry in Scotland and elsewhere, were collected together to fill a leather-bound volume of over a hundred pages of minuscule print. It bore the title *Marriage Rejoicings*, and was probably sold to Frasers the world over. The list of wedding gifts and their givers occupies sixteen pages of sixty-odd lines apiece: advertisement of the forthcoming publication of this book must have constituted a dire threat to those whose thriftiness could be exposed by it.

The bride was whisked away to the bridegroom's highland fastness, Beaufort Castle in Inverness, where she was thought by her sister to have been rather lonely and unsettled to start with.

Three years later, on 17 April 1913, Diana aged twenty married Percy Wyndham, a descendant of the Lords Egremont of Petworth; the grandson of Percy and Madeline Wyndham who were notable Souls – they built a house in Wiltshire and called it Clouds and, rebelling against stuffy Victorian taste, set a trend by decorating it very simply in blue and white; and the son of George Wyndham who was a front-rank politician and supposed to be the handsomest of men. He met his death in action on 15 September 1914, mere weeks after the war began on 4 August.

On the rare occasions on which my mother mentioned

her first husband she would refer to him as 'my Percy', a form of words suggestive of proprietorial pride and love. He was not on the intellectual level of her brother Charles or her brilliant friends such as the Grenfells and Patrick Shaw-Stewart, but seems to have been nice and kind and good-looking. At school he wrote affectionate letters to his grandparents, who treasured and bequeathed them to his widow. His probably descriptive nickname was Perks: could it have been invented by Aunt Laura, who went in for that sort of thing and called her giant of a brother-in-law Hugh Fraser Hugolino?

My grandfather Ribblesdale's immediate reaction to Percy's death was to write: 'My own darling Diana, There is nothing I can say except that I love you very much and all my heart is with you in this day of catastrophe and sorrow for our best and bravest. You know how attached I *am* to Percy – for those we care for can never go away from our hearts and minds – so you will let me and Laura and all those who love you both try to help you in your grief and loss. Your loving father R.'

And again, apparently on the evening of the day the news came through: 'Darling, This is only a little line of love for your awakening – I know a very sad awakening – but believe me it is and will be surrounded by love for him and for you. Your loving R.'

Notwithstanding rumours of Percy's adulterous attachment to a former mistress, the marriage of seventeen months' duration must have been happy, otherwise my grandfather would not have betrayed such acute concern for his daughter.

As soon as she was sufficiently recovered she joined the

hospital unit organised and financed by Millicent Duchess of Sutherland and went out to France, having trained as a nurse for the requisite period to obtain VAD status. Millie Sutherland performed miracles of cutting through red tape and getting wounded soldiers looked after. She was a daughter of Lord Rosslyn and member of a family noted for its charm of manner and waywardness, and after the war married two more husbands and wrote a scandalous novel that reads very like autobiography, *That Fool of a Woman*.

My mother was a born nurse – her other children would be by no means the only ones to agree with me: extremely sympathetic, a better doctor than most, bracing, tireless, pragmatic, and not at all squeamish. For a short time she kept a diary of her life in the places where the hospital functioned, requisitioned private houses and camps under canvas. She and her fellow-nurses go to railway stations and wait for the trainloads of casualties to arrive, and then compete with other organisations for patients. She complains of not being allowed nearer the front line: she thinks the soldiers would have better chances if they could receive medical attention sooner – too many sicken and die during those train journeys. She is undaunted by danger, and curious to hear the sound of the German guns.

When Charles Lister was reported dead just a year after Percy, Laura wrote to Diana, who must have been back in England. The unselfishly distraught tone of her letter bears witness to the suffering already endured by its recipient as well as to that in store for her.

'What *can* I say? I daren't think what this will mean to you. We must try and help Father. I have been with him today, but must go to Simon tonight as these last minutes are so precious – he leaves tomorrow. I don't know how to be away from you during all these terrible hours. God bless and help you.'

AUNT LAURA'S LETTERS to my mother, undated as usual, but seeming to run from 1913, graphically describe the wartime situation of soldiers' wives, sweethearts and relations.

She writes in high spirits before the killing began: 'I can't tell you how overjoyed I am at your happy news. You sweet little darling, I am panting to meet your Percy.'

And probably still in peaceful 1913: 'I feel quite stupid at present – you couldn't *flog* a joke out of me,' because the joking stopped soon afterwards.

She had had two of her five children, Shimi and Magdalen, when the war was declared. Her sister's husband and her husband's brother died within days of each other a few weeks later. News of the fate of her brother-in-law – once her Hugolino – must have reached her first: 'We are all unutterably miserable here as darling Hugh has been killed.'

Her letter about Percy's death is missing. But she responded to missives from my mother: 'Your little letter makes my heart bleed for you . . .' 'Your sad little letters make my heart ache. You are luckily one of the bravest women I have ever known . . .'

[ 41 ]

The Christmas referred to below could be that of 1914, after Percy's death, or 1915, after Charles's: 'I do so hate not to be with thee this cruel Xmas. I know you will be brave and unselfish as you always are, and make Xmas Day as happy as possible for the English soldiers.' And again: 'There will be so many broken hearts this Xmas.'

And on the same lines: 'What can I do for you? Being unable to help you *haunts* me.'

'I heard Colonel Fielding was in London wounded,' she writes, 'so I posted up to see him and ask about Percy's things and who had them. He told me Percy had been perfectly wonderful and his men would have followed him anywhere.'

Then again to my mother in France: 'It must be heartrending work, nursing the dying – I don't know how you do it.'

And warningly: 'Whatever you do, don't get taken prisoner!' In the same vein with a hint of family humour: 'Millie was wise to move you. You might have been killed, or maimed for life which would have been even more trying.'

'What strange and interesting things you have seen and lived through since you went abroad. I sometimes shudder to think how little I have done in this awful war. Life has gone on so smoothly for me, except for sorrowing for you and Perks and Hugh and all the others. I wonder why I should have been immune, whilst you have had to give everything.'

Aunt Laura had a mercurial personality and was not so moved by my mother's plight as not to boss her about.

In the tender letter above she also writes: 'I think you are really becoming as fussy as the Aunts (Lord Ribblesdale's two spinster sisters) over the Mabel question. Do leave well alone, duckie.' Mabel must have been a maid who worked for my mother in the past or present. Her name bobs up repeatedly in the correspondence. 'Mabel's letter is satisfactory – don't fuss any more . . .' 'Don't worry about Mabel – I am quite *positive* she will never leave . . .' 'Don't fret about Mabel – I will cope with her and make her *completely* happy . . .'

'Are you *never* returning to us?' she demands.

The sharper note in Aunt Laura's letters seems to coincide with the end of her 'immunity', for her husband Simon Lovat is 'delighted as he feels he is getting a little nearer the front.'

'Simon definitely leaves in a week. If only only only he were going as anything but a Colonel: next to 1st or 2nd Lieut., no rank could be more dangerous.'

Then: 'Simon leaves on Monday. I feel in despair. But in this cruel hell of war no one must cry before they are hurt. You will know what I am going through.'

And of the event of their parting: 'Simon left me this a.m. I have cried for two days without pause and feel a perfect wreck . . . However, there it is. No tears will bring him back, so I must pull myself together or try to.'

Lord Lovat was born in 1871 and therefore forty-three in 1914. Age was no doubt the reason why he was not permitted to join in the fighting. Eventually he got to the front by dropping in rank from Brigadier to Colonel and taking charge of a hundred picked snipers of Lovat Scouts.

Without him Aunt Laura was melancholy and irritable. While her husband was training with his troops she had followed the drum; and after he had gone, in order to be in an accessible situation in the south of the country rather than in the far north, she continued to rent houses for herself, her children and staff.

She writes: 'I shall be glad to leave this germ-ridden shanty . . .' 'I can't think about the war because of the flea that attacked me in church this morning . . .' 'I am in the almost mortal throes of trying to find a new cook . . .' 'My one joy in the hole we're living in is a dying seagull I picked up on the lawn. It's lying in a basket by my bed and is v. sad and peevish. But I think it will live and I hope love me for ever.'

She had not got a good word to say about some girl called Sybil: 'Fancy Sybil's engaged – after six years of courting . . .' 'Sybil's wedding was quite nice, but as it's Lent there was no music, and of course no bridesmaids. She went away in a hat that was not pretty, sort of mauve and blue, after a fearful entertainment with every member of her family present. I returned here with a terrific cold in the head and am feeling rotten. It's the last wedding I attend.'

She records with amusement this exchange with her four- or five-year-old son: 'Shimi to Self: Oh shut up! Self: Oh Shimi, what an ugly thing to say! Whoever taught you such an expression? Shimi: God.'

But she vents her spleen on my mother: 'You will come back on the 4th, won't you? You keep retarding the date and I am so utterly wretched all alone in this vile town. I feel so seedy too. It would be cruel of you to disappoint me again. You are so terribly unreliable about dates I can never trust you.'

She rubs it in: 'I have no news except that I love you very much which is certainly more than you deserve.'

Perhaps the following sentences in various other letters are the explanation of her edginess, and her exoneration: 'How tragic about Lady Alice's last son . . . Poor Bob died. And yes, alas, Reggie too, though Edward is slowly getting better, I understand . . . Kitty's William is dead, and Betty's son, and Florrie's. England gets sadder every day. And one wonders how one can bear one's own husband going out, when everybody we know seems to have been killed.'

Therefore her prescience was almost like betting on a sure thing: 'I feel desperately worried over Charles. I fear the fighting in the Dardanelles is very violent. Pray God he may escape.'

Her prayer was not answered.

'Father has just heard C has been wounded. The telegram from the Admiralty only said: Regret to say Lieut. C. A. Lister wounded. No indication as to whether it was bad, or where or when or anything. I rushed round to Father who was v. brave and calm. He says all subalterns are doomed, so one can only be thankful when one hears they are wounded. We must pray hard it may be a minor wound, just bad enough to keep him from going out again.'

CHARLES LISTER'S RELIGIOUS epigram deserves to be quoted once more: 'I know now that I shall not die. I do not mean I may not be killed.'

His brother-in-law Simon Lovat wrote home from Gallipoli: 'Everyone speaks of Charles and his great gallantry. His men adored him, and they say he simply did not know the meaning of fear.'

Not many weeks after Charles was duly killed the order was given for the evacuation of the Dardanelles. Thus the campaign in which many valuable lives were lost and nothing was gained came to an end – and with it, I suspect, the euphorically self-sacrificial attitude to the war.

Four long years after it began and my mother was widowed, peace broke out and she re-married.

Her second husband was Arthur Capel, 'Boy' Capel, possibly a remote sprig of the family tree of the Earls of Essex, heir to an industrial empire possibly created by his mother, something of a mystery as she was and still more so his father. An Englishman who was French and lived in France, a Frenchman of English origins, said by some to have Portuguese and Jewish blood in his veins, member of the wartime staff of Clemenceau, author of a thoughtful and influential essay entitled *Reflections on Victory*, Boy was an intellectual, politician, tycoon, polo-player, and is now mainly remembered for having been the lover and financial sponsor of Coco Chanel.

He was also a Roman Catholic, consequently his fiancée had to become one before they could wed: Laura, too, had converted to Catholicism in order to marry into the Fraser family.

I can recall my mother referring to Boy Capel only twice: to say he was very witty and amusing on occasions and if he wanted to be, and to complain that Chanel had refused to return furniture he had lent her. Such reticence might have meant she was either happy or unhappy to have been his wife.

Moreover she was contradictory about her marital circumstances. For years she told me she disliked French people in general and had loathed living in Paris. She then confided in my wife that she had adored the place when she was young and because she was in love with her husband.

And although she would accuse Chanel of not behaving well about that furniture, she cannot have borne much of a grudge against her for any reason, since she continued to buy clothes at her shop long after the connecting link between them was severed.

Chanel has recently caught the predatory eye of popular biography. According to show-business versions of her earlier life, the humbly born but warm-hearted ex-midinette with a touch of genius falls deeply and irrevocably in love with her rich protector, who discards her to marry an aristocratic English girl largely from snobbish and dynastic motives, and regrets it. Yet a French friend of mine who had been friendly with friends of both Chanel and Boy Capel tells me a different story: that she, not he, did the discarding. Apparently at the time in question she was already very successful and wished no longer to be dependent in any sense on a superior gentleman who stole her thunder. Perhaps she had ceased to love Boy and was therefore keen to get rid of him, or perhaps, despite the boggle of history's imagination, she still loved him and so unselfishly as to propel him towards marriage and paternity with a suitable girl of his own class: anyway her effective aim was to reign over her little empire in solitary and undivided state. And afterwards, far from pining for and clinging to him whenever she could, she found she was clung to.

Who knows? The sixty and more years that have elapsed since then provide a negative answer to that question.

My mother's contemporary and friend of our family Joan Altrincham contributes another confusing recollection to the evidence. She remembers visiting my mother in her home in Paris round about Easter: she was alone – minus her husband – and crying in front of a fire that was also out. The causes of her sorrow were her solitude in a foreign land in a festive season, and the fact that she had failed to start a child and had to consult doctors about her infertility.

Since she conceived my sister Anne soon after the wedding, her meeting with Joan must have occurred even sooner. And already Boy was leaving her to her own devices, which were tearful. Was he absent on business? Or seeking or being sought by Chanel? Why was he neglecting her?

And why was she neglecting him? According to Aunt Laura, when my mother became pregnant she returned to England and English doctors to await the birth. She took a house in Embankment Gardens in Chelsea and stayed there for the last months at least of her pregnancy and the first of motherhood. She was always slightly built and may have posed gynaecological problems, so that rest in a restful situation was insisted upon by her advisers; while she certainly would have wished to be near the sister who was her Own Mummy at the appointed hour and in case of emergency. But what was her husband expected to do in the meanwhile?

Anne was safely born. Six months later my mother was pregnant again with June. And Boy Capel was killed in his car.

THE MARRIAGE HAD lasted just on two years, for as much as a quarter of which period husband and wife seem to have lived in different countries. Granted that medical opinion prescribed rest for my mother, she could have rested in Boy Capel's native homeland rather than her own. The conclusion to be drawn is surely that she was sad not only before her maternal yearnings began to be fulfilled, for instance on the day of Joan Altrincham's visit, but afterwards, when she chose to go home by herself to have her child. Her second pregnancy following so soon after the first implies she was faithful to the tenets of her new religion in respect of birth-control – nothing much else.

In 1918 aged twenty-five she had again become a

wife, and now in 1920 aged twenty-seven again a widow.

Incidentally Anne was born in April 1919, and June, her father's posthumous child, in 1920 in the month she was named after.

I used to wonder if their parents' marriage had been made by Aunt Laura insofar as third parties can make matches. I had heard something from someone to this effect; and after all Laura and Boy had been friends, she had worried about her forlorn little sister, was possessed of a dominant and arbitrary disposition, and likely to be eager to catch one more soul for Roman Catholicism. She could well have urged Own Baby with reckless impatience to follow in Own Mummy's religious footsteps. As for the drawback of Boy being more or less a Frenchman, she probably would have pointed out that Listers were francophiles and anyway Diana had lived for long wartime stretches in France; besides it was better to have a husband and potential father of your children than to be a barren widow on the shelf.

But further examination and analysis of my mother's personality caused me to scrap that hypothesis. For she was the most susceptible of women. She was more susceptible and flirtatious than passionate – you could say she was passionately flirtatious – and again more maternal than wifely. And she was simultaneously suggestible, swayed by almost any suggestion put to her, and independent and strong-minded.

Inevitably and without assistance she would have fallen for Boy. She would have been thrilled by his attractive appearance, reputation as lady-killer, membership of a sort of jet set, dashing sportsmanship, success in the field of business, wealth – and especially the fuss he no doubt made of her.

Of course their marriage did not stand much chance of prospering if she entered into it mainly to please her sister; nor if his reason for marrying was because her pedigree rendered her worthy to bear his children, while his true affections belonged to another.

Yet supposing he had loved his wife more truly than he seems to have done, she would then have put the cat amongst the matrimonial doves. Flirtatiousness is by definition fleeting, and flirts are fickle: which would not be acceptable to a man used to having everything his own way, let alone to the Latin temperament. She was British through and through, and insular into the bargain, and inclined to laugh at the melodramatic emotionalism of foreigners. She never was or would be in love with wifehood: she was too proud, self-sufficient, and egoistic, if discreetly. She would not have wanted to live for long in Paris or any town, since she was essentially countrified, or for that matter in France, cut off from her family and old friends. She was nowhere near so much of a francophile as her father and sisters, and would not have consented readily to her children being brought up as French citizens.

The temporary nature of suggestibility was also bound to complicate the issue. Agreeable and accommodating in her amorous enthusiasm at one moment, at the next she was liable to assert her opinions however contrary with some force and stubbornness. And she could be militant in pursuit of her objectives, usually connected with what she believed to be her children's welfare.

[ 51 ]

Perhaps Boy approved of the motherly feelings that induced his wife to abandon him while she was bringing his baby into the world. We all know marriages are not to be plumbed by outsiders. But there seems to have been not much compatibility between them to re-establish, considering his nationality and urban habits, important positions in industry and high finance, which were closed books to her, his intellect as distinct from her intuition, and past or present attachment to a woman who was her exact opposite.

MY MOTHER INHERITED a considerable fortune from Boy Capel. But she must have been rich when she married him. Percy Wyndham's parents were respectively the owner of Clouds and the erstwhile widow of the heir to the Dukedom of Westminster and mother of a Duke of Westminster – Percy's older half-brother was the Bendor Westminster who was to testify to the smallness of the world by having an affair with Chanel.

Whether or not the George Wyndhams had settled any capital on Percy which came his wife's way in the event of his death, or made a settlement on the widow of their only child, I never discovered. But clearly they saw to it that she lacked for nothing during her widowhood, as proved by the fact that during the war years she was already the tenant of Lyegrove.

Shimi Lovat in *March Past* describes staying there

My mother's father Lord Ribblesdale

Lord Ribblesdale
late in life

Lord Ribblesdale
painted by Sargent

My mother's brother Charles Lister, aged twelve,
drawn by Sargent – copy of a portrait of a Lister
ancestor in the background

Charty Ribblesdale in
fancy dress with
powdered hair

Below: My mother on
left and her sister Laura,
known in their early
childhood as The Dolls

My mother and my Aunt Laura with their
mother Charty Ribblesdale

Right: Percy Wyndham

Percy Wyndham with his mother
painted by Sir Philip Burne-Jones

Arthur Capel – Boy Capel to his friends

Three Earls at Ascot Races:
my father in centre with Hugo Londesborough on his left
and Hugh Sefton on his right. The Earldoms of Londesborough and Sefton died with – respectively – my father's first
cousin and his friend, and became extinct

Top: My half-sisters Anne and June, born Capel

Centre: My brother David, my sister Rose and Self on right

Left: Rose

David in uniform of Page to the Duke of Beaufort, and Self in uniform of Page to the Marquess of Cholmondeley, for the Coronation of 1936

A view of the older part of the garden at Lyegrove

The lodge at entrance to the front drive

Front of Lyegrove from the garden

Lyegrove from the raised walk

Lyegrove in early spring from the front drive. This photograph was taken by the estate agents who sold the house after my mother's death. The muddy tracks were made by vans removing the furniture

with his mother and occasionally mine, and visits from his father and other soldiers on leave. The large house was probably rented in order to provide Aunt Laura and her family with a base easier to get at than Beaufort Castle, in which to await their reunions with Lord Lovat. The Lovats may have shared the expenses of Lyegrove, since they were benefiting from it more than my mother who was nursing in France throughout this period. Yet I gather it was mostly my mother's responsibility, and guess that the sisters agreed she should pay for it as she was better off and without commitments.

Boy Capel's finances were another mystery – and time has buried them out of reach of investigation. Gossip has it that his mother, who was of mixed blood and capable and shrewd, rather than his father, whoever his father might have been, built up the businesses he took over and developed. He had interests in coal mining and probably in that side of heavy industry productive of armaments.

He died not knowing of the conception of his second child – he had made no provision for her in his will. My mother's trustees had to institute legal proceedings so that June could be awarded a share in her father's estate.

She rented a house with a fashionable address in London and resumed her tenancy of Lyegrove, now in association with her father and to hunt from. She would move her caravan of children and servants from town to the country and back again as the meteorological and social seasons prompted. By this time she had engaged Nanny Harvey, who was to remain the family's friend and councillor until the day of her death forty years later.

Nanny was always loyal to my mother – she was fond of her, grateful, respected her, and took infinite pains neither to steal nor alienate the affections of her children. But she used to tell the following story. The housekeeper at Lyegrove was a Mrs Simnett. One evening Mrs Simnett came along to the nursery and perching on the high fireguard delivered herself of the sybilline utterance: 'Mrs Capel will soon be telling us she's lonely and has therefore decided to marry again, you mark my words.' Shortly afterwards, Nanny would relate with perhaps a tinge of spinsterish cynicism, my mother announced her engagement to her staff exactly as predicted.

That would have been three years after Boy was killed, driving his car to keep an appointment with someone, but definitely not to meet his wife and ask her for a divorce so that he could marry Chanel – which is the tinselly twist show-business has given the story of his affair with the dressmaker.

The third man she married was my father – the year was 1923.

HE WAS VERE FANE, 14th Earl of Westmorland, commonly known as Burghie, a nickname derived from the courtesy title Lord Burghersh which he along with previous heirs to the earldom had used before inheriting.

He was thirty years old, the same age as my mother; had been educated at Dartmouth, and during the war served in the Royal Navy under Beatty; was a victim of the so-called Geddes Axe which cut down the numbers of professional servicemen and put an end to his naval career; and for the last few years had been concentrating on sport, particularly riding and training race-horses and playing golf – he nearly got into the national golfing team. He was generally acknowledged to have good looks and charm, and was expected in due course to don the popular mantle of the Yellow Earl, Lord Lonsdale.

The phenomenon of the nobleman representing and sharing the interests of the masses, who trust and look up to and regard him with affection, is a thing of the past: film and pop stars and their fans are today's equivalent. Innumerable press-cuttings, photographs and caricatures attest to my father's happy relationship with at any rate the sporting public: he sets fashions with his clothes – loose double-breasted chalk-striped suits, tiepin worn under the knot of a tie; is appointed a director of the Arsenal Football Club, likewise of the Greyhound Racing Association and a variety of horse-racing bodies; is here being cheered past the winning post in his green and white racing colours, and there having a path cleared for him through a congratulatory crowd at a race-meeting; figures with a big cigar at the ringside of prize-fights, sits in the place of honour at banquets for sporting champions, hands out cups and trophies by the score, and is even given some official honorary position by the Tiller Girls, who sit on his knees and cluster round him scantily clad in a publicity still. He loved the Music Hall, was the friend of George Robey and Bud Flanagan amongst others, and in his heyday had a permanent booking of a couple of aisle seats at The Palladium for mid-week evenings. He was an example of the extremes that touch – a patrician in tune with the people. Actually, although he was a crony of the Prince of Wales, later King Edward VIII, who seems to have hero-worshipped him at one time, and was warmly attached to and much sought after by his peers, I think he preferred the company of dustmen to dukes in a manner of speaking, and was most at home with the meritocrats of sport and the theatre.

He may have been as glamorous as his father-in-law and my grandfather Ribblesdale, but in a different way. He was essentially approachable with his easy graceful manners and shining pink face and jollity, clubbable, one of the boys, yet with nothing loud or crude or insensitive or overbearing about him, unpretentious, not needing to pretend or assume, a sportsman in the fullest sense and in the modern classless style followed by his Prince of Wales; whereas Lord Ribblesdale's romantic, brooding, haughty and intelligent countenance and elaborate apparel combine today as yesterday to make him look like the ancestor of aristocracy itself.

My father was the scion of a family with a history at least as long as that of the Listers. The title was already very old when it passed through the female line from the Nevilles to the Fanes in 1624. Our motto is Ne Vile Fano, a pun of the type in fashion in days gone by when there was probably not much else to laugh at: it means in the vernacular Do Not Spit On The Altar, and at the same time From Neville to Fane.

In parentheses and without wishing to cast aspersions on my more distant forbears, the Westmorland in Shakespeare's Henry V who would rather not fight at Agincourt and is accused of cowardice by the King was a Neville.

Not that the Fanes were so brave as to rush to the front of the public stage in the last three and a half centuries. They might not have been clever enough to get there even if they had wanted to, despite their positively scintillating talent for survival. Some hundred and fifty years ago a Westmorland did distinguish himself in the Diplomatic Service, founded the Royal Academy of Music, and fathered my namesake Julian Fane, poet and begetter of Ettie Desborough, the mother of the Grenfells. But otherwise crowns of laurel are almost conspicuous by their absence from family brows.

Earls of Westmorland of yore handed on to their sons and heirs a book in which they wrote words of guidance and advice. There, as time passes, prayers in Latin give way to stodgy homilies in copperplate handwriting and a final scrawled entry to this effect: 'For God's sake keep down ye rabbits in ye park.' Keeping down the rabbits seems on the whole to have stretched familial faculties to the limit. But lack of ambition is not to be mocked: it could have been our saving grace.

The Park referred to above was probably at Apethorpe in Northamptonshire, long the country seat of the Westmorlands, although a precocious and not the last or least extravagant earl built the copy of Palladio's Rotonda, Mereworth Castle in Kent, on his return from the Grand Tour. The family in an inclusive sense owned and own houses elsewhere. Fanes titled and untitled lie beneath funerary monuments in Lincolnshire, Oxfordshire and Berkshire, too – not to mention those issuing from a liaison never legitimised who are buried near the stately homes they acquired stretching right across south-west England, Pythouse, Boyton Manor, and so on.

My father did not spend much of his boyhood at Apethorpe, for it was sold plus contents – the contents very nearly in their entirety – soon after the turn of the century. It has been said his mother Sybil Westmorland brought the family to the brink of ruination: she ordered flowers to fill her enormous country house from a florist in London, and linen by the ton. But magnates on the scale of the Westmorlands are not ruined merely by the follies of their prodigal wives in shops. A likelier story is that during the agricultural slump following the Repeal of the Corn Laws the Lord Westmorland of the day waived the rents of his impoverished tenant farmers and thus – in current jargon – cut off his cash flow: my father also might have forgotten that charity begins at home.

Anyway Apethorpe had to be sold – and then Sybil Westmorland died of grieving for it, or so sentimental gossip claimed.

She was born a St Clair Erskine, like her sister Millicent Sutherland. She was the most beautiful, charming and feckless of the daughters of Lord Rosslyn, and she transmitted many of her characteristics to her elder son.

MY MOTHER HAD several reasons apart from the obvious one to be drawn to my father.

Sybil Westmorland had died prematurely of drink and drugs and no doubt an excess of lovers in 1910. But my mother remembered her coming to stay at Gisburne, an exquisite bejewelled creature in evening dress sweeping into the nursery to kiss the Dolls good night, more fun than any other visitor, their favourite, everybody's favourite, unforgettably delightful.

She did not know until long after my father's death, when I unearthed letters written to Sybil, that her father had been one of her late mother-in-law's lovers. Lord Ribblesdale called Sybil Armida, the name of the siren reigning over the Garden of Enchantment in Tasso's poem *Jerusalem Delivered*. But their affair was short-lived. She seems to have fallen in love with yet another man.

I hope either that the relevant other man was not, or that no vulnerable party knew the other man was, Thomas Lister, Lord Ribblesdale's son and my mother's brother. Lady Curzon, Vicereine of India, writes of 'poor Charty Ribblesdale with both her Tommys in love with Sybil Westmorland.' But Mary Curzon may have been wrong. If she was right, with luck Charty at any rate was less well-informed.

Sybil must have been generous; or – to put it more

bluntly – too good a sport, too eager to please, and kind, co-operative, shallow and amoral to say no. From the word go she broke the laws of love. As a teenager she became engaged to my Westmorland grandfather in the middle of a heavy flirtation with the Duke of Clarence, King George V's elder brother, who was cut to the quick and reproachful in consequence.

But my mother would have been influenced during my father's courtship not so much by rumours of the multiple peccadillos of his mother who had been dead for thirteen years, rather by her own dear vivid memories, and the facts that he was the nephew of Millie Sutherland for and with whom she had done her nursing work in the war, and the first cousin of Millie's daughter Rose – married to the future Lord Dudley – who was her very best girlfriend.

In passing I would mention two meetings I had with Millie Sutherland in Paris long ago. I went to the flat where she lived for years, and have a vague recollection of a tall elegant old lady dressed in grey. Our second encounter was at the British Embassy. We arrived simultaneously for some reception and were admitted together and escorted up the stairs by the butler, who was almost as old as she was: permit me to call him Smithers for the sake of the anecdote. Millie grated out on the staircase: 'We've known a good few ambassadors, haven't we, Smithers – better ones and worse ones, haven't we? But they all go in the end, don't they, Smithers? – Thank God!' The intimacy, gloom and humour of her little speech went down very well with the butler. Her reputation for charm was based partly on her possession of the common touch. Yet by all accounts she was in no way a patch on her sister Sybil. And it was not praiseworthy to hang on to her title and rank through the thick and thin of her two last marriages to plain misters.

Although my father's cousinship with the beloved Grenfells was also bound to appeal to my mother, I suppose such nudges of extraneous encouragement were superfluous. A friendly contemporary of my parents once boasted that she had made their match by telling each in turn that the other was mad about him and her respectively: notwithstanding their reserved natures, and even if it was then the fashion in this country to be sexually cautious, I could never believe the story. My mother was an attractive proposition really in every respect, and my father was often referred to as the ideal representative of the sportsmen of his generation. They were surely not in need of any sort of matchmaking. That she happened to be rich would not have mattered to him as much as to many other suitors. He was completely unmaterialistic, that is to say ignorant of what money meant and where it came from, and anyway was well off in his own right in those days: the proceeds of the sale of Apethorpe were not exhausted. A photograph taken early on in their married life shows them perhaps at a point-to-point: they both wear tweeds, and she brogues with laces criss-crossing round her ankles, and he a Fair Isle jersey and a pin beneath the knot of his tie, and are arm-in-arm and smiling – and thus support my contention that love was a full and sufficient explanation of their union.

In that photograph they appear to have risen above their calamitous honeymoon. They had gone first to a fishing lodge in Scotland lent by the Lovats, where it rained non-stop, then in search of better weather to Biarritz, where it blew a gale. My mother used to give a funny account of how much she had hated it all. She excelled at laughing at herself and in particular at presenting her complaints in a laughable form. But I wonder how well my father, who had the more nervous temperament of the two, stood up to her complaining.

AS NEWLY-WEDS WILL, they hunted for a permanent home. Mereworth Castle complete with exterior friezes of the crest of its creator, the bull's head of the Fanes, happened to be for sale and was one of the houses they considered. But my mother, disregarding its family associations and intriguing history and perfect proportions and so on, rejected it on account of what she considered its dismal atmosphere and the bad luck of its previous owners.

And late in life she confessed that they had got so far as to pay their deposit for the purchase of Ashdown House in Berkshire, which now belongs to the National Trust. But she changed her mind after visiting it on a windy day, decided she could not live in such an exposed situation, and sacrificed the money. She was the only person I have ever known or heard of prepared to kiss goodbye to ten per cent of the value of a house for any reason. She must then have been as blissfully ignorant as my father of the cost of doing as one pleases.

Eventually they bought Lyegrove. The tenant who had sub-let it to my mother in former years, Lady Nesta Wellesley, had disappeared from view by this time; and the Beaufort Estate, having regained control of the property, agreed to sell it to my parents.

It has a climate all its own. Snow can be falling on the big house while the sun shines on the gothic lodge at the bottom of the drive; and I refuse to believe it is less windy than Ashdown House or than almost anywhere else in the British Isles. The site is supposed to have been one of those high points in the landscape from which our forefathers communicated by means of smoke signals; and is moreover on the edge of the plateau above the Sodbury Vale which reaches to the Severn River, Bristol Channel and Atlantic Ocean. Oceanic zephyrs freshened up by the meteorological influence of the North Pole curl over the escarpment and beset Lyegrove at the top. But my mother chose never to register such facts of life there; and for neither the first nor last time she settled for that old favourite of hers, the devil she knew.

My father seems to have taken a back seat throughout these negotiations. He was more interested in stables than houses – and after all the Lyegrove stables were fit for the fussiest horses and their owners. And possibly he was inhibited by my mother buying the place with her money and in her name, although their joint resources were such as to render the question of who paid for what academic.

Major works to their home were set in train. Lord and Lady Ribblesdale as Souls were much preoccupied by interior decoration and furnishings, style and taste – and their daughters likewise. My mother would have taken additional note of the rooms painted the plainest white at Clouds.

With the help of an architect called Kitchen, and the typical antipathy of one generation for the notions of that which preceded it, she banished every bit of Victoriana and installed a new staircase in oak bleached by lime, and after dividing some rooms and joining others together had the majority of them painted and stippled a special soft white. By the application of numerous coats of best oil paint with eggshell finish an effect of light at once reflected and broken by the indentations of the stippling was obtained; and time brought out the umber tint of the oil, so that walls looked like ivory. The process would be ruinously expensive today – it probably was in the 1920s – considering the essential thickness of paint and expertise of the stippler. Yet in my opinion nothing of the sort is prettier; and the passage of fifty-odd years seemed only to improve the appearance of the Lyegrove paintwork.

As for the outside of the house, she allowed my father to have a copy of the porch at Apethorpe erected over the front door, and some lead drainpipes embossed with a W and coronet on each hammerhead. Later she regretted the porch, which was unsuitable.

But Lyegrove never was a period piece or homogeneous architectural gem. A sixth of it – say – was old, part of a grange-like edifice with little mullioned windows dating back to the seventeenth century. A more up-to-date front, and Dutch gables, and one of two projected wings, and a courtyard and bell-tower had been added on. The grey stucco was scored in imitation of dressed stone, and a bit of balustrading crowned the parapet of a roof, and Cotswold stone tiles replaced some of the slates.

Admittedly it might have been better without the porch. But, even when my father had done his worst, the house retained the character my mother looked for and liked in domestic architecture and artefacts. She was unmoved by authenticity and tended to shy away from obvious excellence. Charm was her criterion. Lyegrove not only passed her tests, it provided her with scope to exercise her particular talent for organising disparate and discordant elements into a harmonious whole.

THE STORY OF the creation of her garden is old hat: she told it over and over again, and I have written it for various publications, as indeed she did.

Nevertheless – with apologies – unless I repeat it once more the story of her life, especially its later stages, would be incomplete and even incomprehensible.

Horticulturally speaking, my mother was the child of the renowned half-blind gardener Miss Jekyll. That is to say she was in favour of a formally planned garden with architectural features, the sharper edges of which should be softened by profuse and multi-coloured planting of herbaceous borders, roses, clematis, etc. Carefully studied carelessness was the method, and the aim modest and partially ruined grandeur beautified by flowers.

The convention rebelled against by Gertrude Jekyll and her frequent collaborator Edwin Lutyens was a garden in the classic French style consisting of a geometric pattern of paths and neat ankle-high greenery near the house, and farther vistas of a self-consciously tamed landscape.

The convention that has superseded Miss Jekyll's is on show at Vita Sackville-West's Sissinghurst, a series of cottage-sized gardens planted in a sophisticated and non-natural way, for instance one colour.

My mother had done no gardening at Lyegrove while only a tenant there. But she was interested in the subject, and admiring and envious of the arum lilies filling her sister's flowerbeds at Beaufort Castle.

All she seemed to have was a kitchen garden surrounded by a tumbledown wall with a green-painted door in it, which was awkwardly situated to one side of her new home.

But Lyegrove also had a folly of an ivy-clad summer-house on a terraced walk. When the ivy was removed she discovered, somehow attached to the building, a pair of remarkably fine pillars with shell-like niches carved out of the stones, and manorial balls aloft. She moved them so that they flanked an entrance down steps into the old kitchen garden, where a central lily-pool of an intricate shape was excavated and yew hedges planted to divide the area into quarters. Flowers and shrubs replaced the vegetables, although the apple trees were left in peace to blossom prettily and bear their rather inedible fruit.

Years passed, those years which are not counted by true gardeners like my mother, and in 1933 or thereabouts she yielded to the ambitious impulse which seems to be another of the distinguishing marks of the genuine breed. She decided to extend – take in the bit of paddock beyond the present garden. Again she had recourse to the summerhouse: she moved it stone by stone – at a cost of £120 – to the end of an avenue of ornamental white cherries. Then she dug out two sunken rectangles, piled up the excess earth for raised herbaceous borders, built hundreds of yards of retaining walls, and finished off the job with enclosing hedges of yew.

I remember these developments, which took place probably in my seventh year. I remember the numbered blocks of Bath stone of the summerhouse lying on the ground before they were re-stacked in order to form the walls and graceful arches of the focus of the so-called spring garden; and the digging and the morass of mud.

But when the rough contractors departed the Lyegrove gardeners set to, and according to my recollections soon had everything under control and tidy. There must have been five or six gardeners: not too long ago I came across photographs of them and the garden in my young days. The head-gardener Mr Wootton looks like the managing director of a thriving company, bespectacled and with a stubbly moustache, dignified, energetic and sleek. The season is summer: he is wearing a stiff collar and tie, matching waistcoat and trousers of striped worsted material, and a green baize apron – and I think his sleeves are rolled up. The lowliest of the work-force is Mr Harris, a gnarled diminutive peasant in a shapeless tweed hat, whose concertina-ed grey whipcord trousers are tied below the knee with string, revealing huge boots with bulbous toecaps. The lawns are comparable to billiard tables, the hedges so vertical and right-angled as to resemble theatrical props, the flowers stand to attention, and surely no weed would have dared to intrude.

The doubt in my mind in respect of Mr. Wootton's sleeves is due to my knowing he did no hard manual labour. His sleeves might just as well have been rolled down and fastened with cuff-links. His job was inclusively to order others to dig and sweat; formulate plans in his office; tap the pots of flowers in the greenhouses and judge by the sound if he should water them; have certain pots brought into the house on a sort of bier carried by two men every week or fortnight; arrange said pots in large copper receptacles in such a way that the blooms appeared to be growing out of moss; and quarrel daily with the cook about kitchen produce.

He had also helped to fix the shape of my mother's garden for the next half century.

The site of the two horticultural enclosures was never perfect in her and no doubt others' eyes. She would have liked her garden, rather than the gravel sweep for cars and the drive, to be in front of the house, although she grew to love the stretches of rough grass on either side of the drive where snowdrops, daffodils, tulips and cow-parsley flourished and multiplied under the canopy of the beech trees.

But she was sufficiently satisfied to leave the bones of bricks and mortar, stones and hedges undisturbed. From now on she changed nothing, except the combinations of the colours of her flowers. It was her special gift as gardener, her ability continually to refine and improve her colour schemes. I think her garden became internationally famous more on account of its subtle colouring than its other charms such as well-proportioned layout and serenity.

1934 AND 1935 must have been good years for my parents.

They had been married for a decade; their three children were safely born, my brother David, myself, and the youngest Rose; and Anne and June were growing into lovely girls; and Lyegrove was more or less as they had wanted it to be; and its master and mistress in early middle-age were healthy and wealthy, handsome, popular – in short, in those worldly words, loved and envied.

They hunted in winter. In summer they rented houses in London for the social season, and packed all the children off for a fortnight by the sea and maybe joined them briefly. They went to stay in statelier homes and had people to stay, snapshots of whom playing tennis, croquet, golf, or lolling on long chairs in the garden, or standing by their spotlessly clean limousines in front of the copy of the Apethorpe porch, or at meets of the Beaufort Hounds or race-meetings or horse-shows or other local functions, were duly pasted into my mother's scrapbooks.

She wrote at length of her five children in those books, recording the first witticisms they lisped, and scholastic and sporting successes and failures, as well as charting their progress photographically. She also wrote her letters in the mornings in the drawing-room, where the glass drops of candelabra on a table in a window acted like prisms to the southern sunshine and projected rainbow hues in every direction. She was always active and busy: my memories of her at this period are mostly of the hour or so she spared us younger ones in the smoking-room after tea.

We saw even less of my father. While we were in the smoking-room, he would probably be telephoning in his study next door; or he might have invited some friend in there for a chat and to get away from the noisy brats. He had given up riding and training race-horses by now; but the stables were full of hunters and our ponies. He was often bent on the pleasure of sport, and absent also in London, where he was half-heartedly a businessman and had his charitable interests, not to mention his social engagements and commitments.

The agency that allowed my parents so much liberty and leisure was their staff – or more fundamentally the money enabling them to employ two chauffeurs, four or five in the stables, three housemaids, three in the kitchen, two in the pantry, a nanny and nurserymaid, lady's maid, governess, and secretary who spent twenty-four hours in the house monthly and paid all the bills, plus gardeners.

Domestic service earned itself a bad name. But Lyegrove was a nice place for those who did the serving, too. Sooner or later and for one reason or another they were all dispersed: most of them corresponded with my mother until death intervened, or they would return on sentimental pilgrimages, and the burden of their recollections was that the period of their servitude had been a kind of golden age.

The snobbish formality below stairs was much worse than any consciously practised above. The upper servants, housekeeper, cook, head parlourmaid in charge of my father's clothes, lady's maid, and visiting counterparts, ate in a room so sacrosanct as to be called simply The Room, set apart from the Servants' Hall. Interdepartmental rivalry was rife: the relentless skirmishing between the kitchen, wanting younger tenderer vegetables and more of them, and the garden, reluctant to ruin its show of produce, was by no means unique. And the wastefulness of the whole operation was a bit shocking.

On the other hand the bosses were gentry. Perhaps only the upper classes find it difficult to define a gentleman: everybody else knows a gentleman is someone who has plenty of cash and dispenses it liberally. The evidence is that my parents veered towards the opposite extreme to that of spoiling the ship for a ha'porth of tar. They made it obvious there was more than enough money to go round.

And a rich household like a rich country is easy to govern. It would have been hard for a servant at Lyegrove not to come to the conclusion – especially during the years of economic depression and slump – that he or she was lucky to have a well-paid secure job in a warm comfortable house in beautiful surroundings, considerate and protective and not very demanding employers, lots of time off and sumptuous fare prepared by a team of experts.

Life could have been and in some cases probably was lazy; but our servants were not so harassed as to forget to be proud – and pride would not let them lower standards. Arts were practised which are now completely or almost lost, boning shoes, for example, or cleaning and whitening leather breeches, or goffering, or folding linen napkins into festive shapes. Likely lads and lasses had the fun of learning how to do things properly and later the wages of having learnt. There was congenial company, and much flirting, and romantic and even matrimonial opportunity.

The children of my parents' employees seemed as a rule to rise up and cross class frontiers. Tycoons from distant continents, chairmen of companies, engineers, doctors would come to tell my mother they had sprung from the soil of Lyegrove and were respectively the boys of Jack in the stables, or Edith the tweeny, or Florence the scullery-maid, or May and the van-driver who used to deliver the bread. Edith and Florence themselves in their older age would arrive at our annual garden fete in smart cars and clothes and refer to their youth in harness at Lyegrove as the happiest time of their lives. Once an ex-employee asked if her daughter could work for my mother for two years in order to find out how a house ought to be run and a lady should behave.

I record these facts partly by way of tribute to my parents, and partly to express surprise that such domestic work is spurned today by English men and women.

It would always have been amongst my choices of alternative career. Service is never demeaning – to live is to serve somebody or something: on the contrary it is in itself the most natural, fulfilling and elevating of occupations. And how pleasant as it were to be adopted by and become an honorary member of a kind responsible family!

BUT IN THE mid-thirties egalitarian fate must have noticed my parents' superfluity of blessings.

The first piece of bad luck it dished out to redress the balance of the good was my father's illness and Hugo Londesborough's death.

My father had spent his youth at a house called Blankney in Lincolnshire, now burned down, then the seat of Lord Londesborough and his wife born a Fane, whose son and heir Hugo was his best friend. The reason was that after Apethorpe was sold and Sybil Westmorland died, my Westmorland grandfather re-married and shed the burden of the four children bearing his name by depositing them in the homes of relations.

They looked like twins or at any rate brothers, my father and the Uncle Hugo I recall: they had the same reddish complexions and thinning fair hair going grey at the temples, and were the same height and build, and cut similar handsome figures in the tremendously checked and long and loose tweed jackets they wore in the country.

Hugo had been military whereas my father was naval, and remained single until he was in his forties. According to my mother he was a somewhat solitary and depressive individual inclined to spend every spare moment reading thrillers. He was a Master of Foxhounds, he continued to share my father's interest in horsemanship and racing, and when he stayed at Lyegrove in the non-hunting summer months they would ride together – I expect he was trying the horses. They seemed to be as close as ever, they shaved and bathed in the morning in my father's bedroom – we used to listen to the backchat and laughter. They proved their affinity perhaps by falling ill with pneumonia simultaneously.

It was often a mortal disease before the invention of antibiotics. It killed Uncle Hugo. My father's recovery posed the question of whether he would die of the shock of hearing the first cousin he loved had not survived.

He withstood it. But he was in a wretched state of health as a result of his fight for life and his grief. Convalescence in the sunshine of Italy was prescribed. A nurse who had helped him to pull through agreed to take him there. But he did not like the look of her in civilian clothes, and the better he felt the less he enjoyed her company, so he cut short the trip and hurried home.

At least retrospectively my mother suffered pangs of guilt for not going with him to Italy. Of course she would have had cast-iron excuses for staying at home: maternal duties, children's holidays and so on. Yet I suspect she had already reached the stage of refusing to join in his social activities.

The underlying cause of her careless and even callous behaviour, which was not characteristic, surely was that he had shown himself to be not just the heavy drinker – so masculine and attractive to women – of their earlier married days.

[ 74 ]

No one knows anything about addiction to drugs such as alcohol. I would advance the theory nonetheless that my father's noted ease of manner was not all that easy to project, and his reputation for charm cost him quite an effort to maintain; and as he grew older his convivial but highly strung temperament and resources of sheer energy were therefore subjected to increasing strain, which he could only relieve by having a quick one or two or three. The consequences could be socially embarrassing for his abstemious wife, and the more distressing because he did not have the sort of powerful constitution that can cope with or actually benefit from the intake of hard liquor. His digestion was adversely affected, and before long his nervous system showed signs of damage.

Again, psychology as yet has no infallible advice to offer someone who would love to free another from his or her dependence on a drug. Treating it as an illness may have superseded the old idea of treating it as a crime. But so to sympathise with and care for dependency as to salve the counter-productive bad conscience of whoever is dependent can be beyond the depleted strength of a spouse, already exhausted by trying to keep the matrimonial situation on the rails of normality.

Lots of people would corroborate my claim that both my parents had fine qualities. But if my father was a trifle spoilt and weak, my mother had a tendency to pity herself, perhaps developed by her experiences of tragedy. She suffered a deep sense of injury when her husband carried on doing what she had asked, told and entreated him not to do; and seized her chances to rub it in that he had added to the long list of undeserved wrongs visited upon

[ 75 ]

her. She punished him further by being as un-co-operative as she understood him to have been.

I suppose her attitude was the opposite of remedial, and bound to drive him to drown the new sorrow of her displeasure: but only those not afraid to throw stones in their glass houses would say so.

She always meant well, was at her best with ill people, and more than a good nurse, even a bit of a healer; and he was the kindliest man, decent, gentle in every sense, and devoted to her and his family. Between them they still could not solve the problem which was soon to plague others, too.

No doubt the issue was confused by the ambiguity of marital relations. My father erred doubly by propping up bars with sportsmen at sporting fixtures and elsewhere, thus sacrificing my mother's goodwill and drinking more because he had sacrificed it. But my mother erred in seldom subordinating her interests to his, and in reiterating that she would rather be dead than trail round a golf-course, for instance, or mix with his gang of rough diamonds. Perhaps he drank to assert himself and in an attempt not to be enslaved by the covert imperialism of her personality. And perhaps she was anxious to preserve her separate identity, and used what and where and with whom he drank as pretexts not to lose it in his shadow.

More simply they may have been incompatible – a bitter pill for their mutual fondness to swallow.

The fact beyond argument is that they carried the old matrimonial struggle for supremacy and survival to the point at which outsiders cease to comprehend the protagonists' motives.

[ 76 ]

I would just repeat that he must have been sad to have to go to Italy without her, as she was sad not to have gone with him.

Regrets that husbands and wives impose on one another are not good for marriages.

A YEAR OR so later the solicitor in charge of my mother's financial affairs died and was found to have embezzled roughly a third of her fortune.

She was still rich by most standards. But trouble with the Lyegrove roof or drains, or dry rot or death-watch beetle in its timbers, or any of the major ills that homes are heir to, could cost more capital to rectify than she had to spare – or now possessed.

And my father was not the help he probably should have been. He had not kept a sufficiently sharp eye on her money; and under the impression that they had so much he had squandered a large part of his own.

Financially he was halfway down the slippery slope. The debts incurred when he dabbled in training race-horses, and merely by living in his habitual and open-handed manner, had been paid by the entailed family trusts of which he was the present beneficiary: his trustees' condition for doing so was that his life should be insured for the sum in question and he should pay the premiums of the insurance policy. In other words they coughed up: the insurance company would reimburse them when he died; and they would be able to hand over to his son the full value of the trusts in their stewardship. Meanwhile he had less capital and less revenue deriving from it, but the extra outgoings of those premiums to meet. He had to keep on repeating the process which brought him relief in the shorter term and ever nearer ruin in the longer.

He peeped into the abyss – familiar to many, the more frightening in his case because he had not known it was there – between income and expenditure. Too many of his connections with commercial companies were nominal: for not doing much he was paid ditto, while his charitable work cost him a packet, as did every other activity and recreation he enjoyed. Making money was a mystery to him, something like the Indian rope trick. He had been brought up to take the blasted stuff for granted. He was popular with all classes of men and women partly because he did not judge by monetary criteria.

He could do nothing to help himself and his wife except bet on horses which usually came in nowhere, but might win and put both of them back on their financial feet: in short he carried on as before.

My mother seems not to have held his ineffectuality against him. Perhaps she accepted the fact that by definition glamour such as his does not come cheap. Again, her view of money was so hazy that she was amazed later on when her children actually earned some. But whereas he evinced an optimistic streak by pouring more and more money down the punter's drain, she was rendered chronically pessimistic by and about their economic prospects – she realised her latent terror of penury.

[ 78 ]

She is unlikely to have suffered from it before: she had no practical reason to. Yet her Lister grandfather had ruined the family and her father had been penniless until he married the daughter of Sir Charles Tennant – possibly in her youth she contracted a fear of poverty resembling one of those infections which only incubate into illness in special circumstances and after a long lapse of time. Theft on a grand scale of money belonging to her and her Capel daughters was the agency bringing it out. Her future wariness in all matters related to finance was traceable to the dirty trick played on her by her late solicitor, a man at the top of his professional tree, her trusted adviser and personal friend, who had run an estate in Yorkshire on his ill-gotten gains and had the effrontery to invite June to stay there: June had gone and enjoyed herself unknowingly at the expense of her inheritance. What translated the chagrin of the cheated into deeper emotions and canalised the apprehensive side of my mother's temperament really for the rest of her life was Lyegrove – her dread of not being able to afford to remain at Lyegrove.

Sophisticated as she was, she had the primitive attachment of a peasant to the soil of her home. She loved it. She had created her garden on and of it. She would and did talk until the cows came home of leaving the place and moving into something smaller. But she clung on, limpet-like. That she could sway and wobble so indecisively on the edge of departure was in reality an indication of how firmly rooted she had become.

She was not wrong to worry all the same. Lyegrove was far beyond my parents' joint and reduced means.

Then war broke out in the nick of time and the style of life of the family had to change completely.

MY FATHER VOLUNTEERED and was recalled into the navy. Anne married, and June went to do war-work in another part of the country. The able-bodied men employed by my parents joined the services, while some of the women and girls signed on in local factories, one left to look after her mother, and the rest receded into the shadows of the times. Our horses and ponies were disposed of and the stables loaned to the government for storage. And the greenhouses were closed down for the duration and the garden got out of hand.

Thus, with none of the friends who had served us being sacked to my knowledge, the bill for wages, bed and board was reduced.

Nanny remained at her post: in 1939 Rose was only eight, I was twelve and still centred on the nursery in my holidays from prep school, and David would have been fifteen. Somebody from Badminton stepped into the breach in the kitchen and cooked us the unpalatable things we ate in the war, Woolton Pie and snoek; somebody else must have helped to clean the house; and an unfit pensioner pottered round in the garden – I have no recollection of how he mowed the lawns without petrol for the mower.

And the truth is my mother preferred it – we all know truth is stranger than fiction.

The popular materialistic myth which tells us luxury is the universal ideal and objective was exploded at Lyegrove. Socialistic threats to curtail the pleasures of the idle rich are no more than the fantasies of envy in the context of my family history.

This new war should have made my mother miserable. She had more reasons than most people to tremble at its declaration, having been so sorely wounded in the region of the heart by the last one. Her husband was again involved, if in a non-combatant role owing to his age, and her sons might grow to qualify for the fighting. And soon she was repetitively mourning the dead and concerned for casualties and prisoners, and distributing messages of condolence and encouragement.

But – setting aside the relief she may have felt to be having a sort of holiday from marriage – she positively enjoyed her altered circumstances. Instead of having breakfast brought to her in bed, she ate it downstairs with twice the appetite. Instead of having to choose her clothes every day from full wardrobes, and almost being dressed by her lady's maid, she got rid of so many clothes that choice was easy, and was delighted not to be fussed over for an hour but able to dress in a few minutes. She never doubted she would rather drive herself in a car than be driven; shop than be shopped for by servants with her money to burn; stick to her meagre food ration than be stuffed with four enormous meals daily; and, as they say, control her destiny.

And she willingly paid the price of her liberation from

her employees, and independence. She was happier to scrub floors than she had ever been to strut over them. She was pleased to discover she was more capable than anyone had supposed: she took the duties formerly done by the monthly secretary in her stride. She might have been a goose academically and in the opinion of her scholarly siblings long ago: she was an eagle of efficiency. The metaphorical orphan of the storm of bereavement, who had needed to be spared disagreeable and upsetting emotions, the pitiable darling enfeebled by disaster who had had to spend an hour or two resting on her bed in the afternoons, developed into the relative dynamo of energy and tower of strength of the remainder of her life.

Paradoxically, no longer being indulged was her chance to indulge herself. Joy through work was only half of her self-indulgence. Joy through saving, not spending money, not bringing noticeably nearer that evil day on which angels with flaming swords would evict her from Lyegrove, was at least as intense. Now that the family was split up and no guests came to stay, the house was unquestionably too big – it was ridiculously so – and likewise expensive. But it was much less expensive than before; and the slower it ticked over the lower the costs. She reduced her personal expenditure to virtually nil. Asceticism was no effort, she found; while thriftiness stirred some previously dormant element of her character. You could say, notwithstanding her inability to curb her generous impulses, she did not have all that Scottish blood in her veins for nothing.

Unfortunately for both my parents my father's health broke down under the unaccustomed stress of his naval responsibilities, he was invalided out of the service, and returned to a home changed almost beyond recognition.

IT GRIEVES ME to recall the clouds gathering over my parents' heads. A memory of a happy interlude pierces the gloom – I was going to say it occurred in 1940, after my father's homecoming, but the definite presence of Anne unwed, and of June and some members of the staff, argues in favour of the early autumn of 1939.

Anyway, on a drowsy afternoon of sunshine and the subliminal buzz of insects a squadron of armoured cars roared up the drive. The squadron leader – a captain or major in a cavalry regiment which had been motorised – and several of his officers also belonged to what seemed to my brother and me the legion of our sisters' 'young men': it turned out they were Anne and June's friends, even suitors, visitors to Lyegrove in former piping times, and acquaintances of my parents. They were on manoeuvres, they explained. Could they bivouac in the grounds until the following morning?

Permission was granted with ready patriotism. The armoured cars were hidden from aerial view under the leafy beech trees in the drive, and covered nonetheless with camouflage netting, and some small tents were put up and pegged down amongst my mother's precious bulbs. But the weather was so warm and the night promised to be so fine that the majority of soldiers decided to sleep in the open on their ground-sheets. Water hot and cold, for washing and making tea, was fetched from the house, and preparations for an evening meal set in train.

By now David and I were in a ferment of excitement. We had greeted the officers who once had been or still were kind to us for our sisters' sakes, shown soldiers the way to the kitchen and various water-taps, ushered them into lavatories, and watched them park the vehicles which especially appealed to the innate paranoia of childhood by being semi-impregnable. We asked numberless blood-thirsty questions about offensive weapons and military life in general. They embodied our ideal of masculinity, these muscular resourceful cheery men in uniform, armed to the teeth and unafraid of spending the night out of doors, let alone the Germans.

The group having drinks on the terrace called us. One of the officers was demonstrating his personal and surely illegal armament. He had got it in America, he said, where gangsters used the same sort of thing. It consisted of a heavy automatic pistol and skeletal metal stock which could be joined together for shooting from the shoulder. It was gleaming steel-blue in colour, and fitted into a beautiful leather case lined with red baize.

Would he fire it, please? Would he show us how it worked – would he shoot something with it? Please! But Anne and June did not want him to; and he told us he was sorry – he was keeping every bullet he had for the enemy.

My parents were there, laughing at the bragging and ragging, and probably touched as well by the high spirits of such boyish champions of our freedom from tyranny.

[ 84 ]

My father strolled down the drive to chat with the other ranks and be sure they had everything they needed.

I peer back over the years and see his rubicund benevolent face and grace of movement and indescribable stylishness. He had the rare sartorial gift of making clothes look better on him than they would on anyone else – he would have been the best male model, and indeed did figure continually in *The Tailor and Cutter*. On this occasion he wore an open-necked shirt of white ribbed material, golfing jacket unzipped, and the somewhat baggy trousers that concealed the thinness of his long elegant legs which only came into their own in hunting boots. Later that evening he changed into his old tobacco-brown velvet smoking-suit.

The officers were invited to dinner. Time has not yet succeeded in expunging the scene from my memory. The particular hour must have been just before dusk and the drawing of blackout curtains, say nine o'clock. The low red sun in a greenish sky shone through the trees of the grove and along the western verge of the drive, slashing the lawns and the encampment beyond them with twilight rays. There was not a breath of wind, and smoke rose vertically from the bonfires in the driveway round which the soldiers huddled: had my mother sanctioned their horticultural vandalism? The intense silence of the countryside as night falls – that somehow loud silence reigned, broken by the sudden shrieks of swallows and the premature hoot of an owl, and by the mutter of voices near and far and laughter.

David and I were still on the loose. We pressed our noses against the panes of the windows of the hall. The

[ 85 ]

silver candelabra with the red paper shades singed in places by the flames of candles were spaced along the length of the oak refectory table. My mother sat at one end and my father at the other – and my sisters glittered and flirted in between. The five or six guests were flushed not just with military fitness by now, also with food and wine. Their lively optimistic conversation and the obbligato of female contributions drifted through the open front door and mingled with the distant muted chorus from the drive.

It was impressively romantic and traditional. It might have been a painting entitled: Nobleman Entertains Soldiery Before The Battle – it was like the Duchess of Richmond's Waterloo Ball on a small scale.

But on second thoughts it certainly occurred soon after the war started, that is before my father rejoined the navy and was invalided out and lost his confidence, and any sort of entertaining at Lyegrove created insuperable difficulties.

And after all it was not such a happy occasion, considering that two of the men who sat down to dinner were killed, and my father himself did not have very long to live.

HE COULD NOT get used to the changes wrought in his home during his absence: the smoking-room and his study beyond it closed, and the big drawing-room only opened up in summer, and the so-called schoolroom where we children had been taught our first lessons turned into a sitting and dining-room combined.

And where was the staff of yesteryear, where were the integral parts of the sort of little community he had been bred more to belong to than rule, the dependents he depended on, the dear friends he was accustomed to living with and being looked after by?

Apethorpe and Blankney, the homes of his youth, had been palaces compared with Lyegrove, even Lyegrove in all its pre-war splendour. The Londesboroughs had had a large house and land in Regent's Park in London to which they took a herd of cows and a flock of sheep to keep them going through the summer season. My father had already compromised and settled for a much more modest establishment in which to bring up his family than he was brought up in. And either because he was getting on in years and stuck in the rut of his ways, though still only fiftyish, or more likely because he was not well, he was unable to move with the times – he had reached his limit. He would have been glad to lay down his life in the national interest: his own and especially his loved ones' sacrifices on the domestic front were another matter. He hated having to watch his wife perform menial tasks, however cheerfully. He must also have felt that her toil was the consequence of his failure to provide for her adequately.

He was between millstones of his own making. His health might have stood up to the rigours of the navy if he himself had not undermined it. By breeding and by training he was cut out to serve his king and country loyally, and had not managed to do so. He could scarcely bear to witness the Cinderella story in reverse as acted by his wife: which no doubt prompted the reflection that if he had taken better care of her money and not squandered his, Lyegrove even now would be re-populated and once again astir with helpful activity. Moreover he would not be at the mercy of her new passion for economy.

He had nothing to do. I mean that wartime restrictions and lack of cash prevented him from doing almost everything he enjoyed. He would wander disconsolately into the overgrown garden and round by the leaky greenhouses and down the disintegrating drive and past the empty stables and back to the house with its shuttered rooms and deserted offices. He had friends everywhere and could not get at them: travel by car was rationed – he loathed trains – and as he was apt to say my mother would not invite a cat into the house. Race-meetings and golf-courses were out of reach physically, and the metropolis financially. The scraps of food on offer he could not bring himself to eat, or else he could not digest them. He was never much of a reader, and in the evenings, in particular the interminable winter evenings in the country during which my mother would stitch away contentedly at her needlework after a busy day, his sole occupation was listening to the usually bad news on the wireless, apart from long-distance telephoning, which was costly and frowned upon.

He was no gardener – he was not encouraged to create mayhem in my mother's flowerbeds. But he took to woodman's work, felling trees and splitting and sawing them into logs. And he invested in a motorbike: it seemed

[ 88 ]

to make his petrol ration go further, and riding it was the next best thing to sitting on a saddle on the back of a horse. He formed the motorbike section of the local Home Guard and paraded on Sunday mornings in khaki rather than in navy blue.

The drawback was that increasingly often he would have to ring up from wherever he had ridden and ask to be fetched by car. His search for opportunities to exercise his talent and cast the spell of his charm, the requisite of which was an audience, landed him in the bars of hostelries, clubs and pubs. He liked strangers, who were more mindful of their own business than his as a rule, and to meet them on the neutral ground of commercial premises. But the after-effects of such sociable sprees in the longer term were the loss of his nerve to ride his motorbike or for that matter drive anywhere, in case he should find it difficult to get home – and frustration, restlessness, more drinks and cigarettes and cigars and pipefuls of tobacco, the deterioration of his health, which now scarcely permitted him to swing an axe of an afternoon, and ever closer confinement within the four walls of Lyegrove.

His last resort was his favourite pastime – betting on horses. Far from restoring the fortune he had largely frittered away on representatives of the equine race, or his self-respect, the ungrateful beasts always carrying more money than he could afford nearly broke him.

MY MOTHER COULD not cope with it: who can?

I do not mean to strike too pessimistic a note. Evidence supports the possibility of rooting out of a temperament its tendencies to be excessive and addictive. And people cured of the sickness are probably better than they were before they contracted it – at least they are inclined to live longer.

But there seems to be no excitement quite like that of going too far, and everybody knows forbidden fruit tastes sweetest. The cruel truth may be that such pleasures are irreplaceable and existence without them is so dull as to be hardly worth the effort.

My mother lacked the previous experience which would have given her a chance to nip the whole business in the bud. She also lacked the will and had no wish to turn her dear husband into a different sort of person. Her mentality of a survivor just could not stretch to comprehension of his world-weariness and self-destructive streak.

Realising she was reacting belatedly she over-reacted. She banished alcohol from the house or tried to. She uttered provocative warnings when he went out and re-proaches when he came in. She rebelled against his prodigal folly and her inability to restrain it. In short she behaved naturally enough, if not with the forbearance advocated by experts resident in ivory towers.

My father had taken part in tough sports, and at a cursory

glance looked like the tough sportsmen he had been pleased to associate with. But his drinking at once masked and betrayed his diffident sensibility. Alcohol was the agent that enabled him to rise above it and be or believe that he was the life and soul of every party. He probably inherited his addictive inclinations from his mother; but owing to the prudishness of his parents' generation he did not discover the cause of her premature death until too late for it to serve as a cautionary tale. He no longer wanted a drink: he needed drink more and more as it were to keep his nerves quiet. At the same time he was full of good intentions, and eager to please and win approval and love.

With hindsight and in the perspective of objectivity the consequences are foreseeable. He hated not only to hear he had done wrong, but to have done it. Somehow he had to ease the strain of being and saying sorry – he had to wash down those hunks of humble pie. But to do so in his customary way was another offence according to his better half.

And certain general laws in this unhappy context began to operate.

The days of wine and roses are definitely numbered: sooner or later they turn into days of wine and a crown of thorns. Intemperance when sober never will face up to the damage done in its cups, especially to its nearest and dearest and more especially its children who are too young to understand and make allowances. Again intemperance never assumes responsibility for the multiplication of its maladies, or acknowledges that it is suicidal: the nourishment in alcohol puts off the evil hour. And the majority of doctors skulk about like the rest of us in this moralistic area of advising someone to live or die.

My father could not or would not bridge the gap between his past and present. The darling of fortune had diminished into a sort of prisoner of war and, now peace had broken out, an ailing peer consigned to obscurity, a back number in the backwoods, the hole in his wife's pocket in a manner of speaking, and apparently the worse half of their marriage. His annual income was only a few pounds more than the cost of the cigarettes and tobacco he never stopped smoking. Whether or not he arrived at a conscious choice in respect of his future, he got the message through to her that he was not going to change.

I called them incompatible. Perhaps their deeper incompatibility was that they were too similar to complement each other. Her nature was as kind as his, and she too seems to have drawn conclusions from the unkindness inherent in their responses to the situation. Even for the best of reasons she ceased to bully him. After all she could not bring herself to convince him she meant business and induce the terror of rejection and divorce, desertion and isolation that might have compelled him to try to survive.

She cared for and then nursed him lovingly, indulging his every wish, until he died in 1948.

I WAS TWENTY and had not been summoned to his bedside during his shortish last illness: in fact I had not set eyes on him for about a year.

The mood at Lyegrove when I arrived there was realistic: his death could not be quite so bad a thing for my mother or for himself as his life had been latterly.

But his funeral summoned in me at any rate contrary emotions and regrets. Race-course bookies and tipsters, jockeys, erstwhile grooms of his and other employees, naval mariners not as able-bodied as they used to be and members of his motorbike section in the recent war, licensed victuallers and barmaids, bottle-nosed characters of both sexes and sports of every description, had travelled more or less far and paid money to bid him goodbye – not to mention the congregated grandees. Men shook my hand hard, and women kissed me tearfully, because I was the son of their friend, heart-throb, hero, boss, benefactor, a perfect gentleman, they assured me, the best of the bunch, and one of the old school whose like would never again be seen.

Those tempted to dice with death as he did should be warned that posthumously, also, they will put pressure on their offspring, who in time will take an increasingly charitable view of the late parent in question and be dogged by memories of the chances he or she missed to show filial affection.

Again victims of their own excesses might be restrained by the realisation that by giving up the ghost they subject their spouses or whoever is meant to be in charge of them to the same sort of painful process of coming to terms with the proof of failure and with remorse.

In her old age, my mother told me: 'I'm glad now I didn't leave your father.'

I think she never quite emancipated herself from the

incubus of the arguments not as to what he had done, but as to how she could and should have prevented him doing it.

Meanwhile she was preoccupied by a matter always close to her heart, if not closer than her third and last marriage from which she was released in material terms.

What about Lyegrove?

It was even more obviously too big for the widow she had again become, and too expensive with each inflationary day that passed. Four of her five children had their own homes to live in, and responsibilities in London and elsewhere; and Rose would soon flutter from the nest, and then Nanny intended to retire to an eventide home. Everybody advised my mother not to stay on.

The result was that she stayed. Obstinacy and procrastination combined together to win her another reprieve. She could have claimed she was not in a fit state to move anywhere. She and my father were fifty-five when he died – they were married for twenty-five years. For at least ten of the years of that quarter of a century she had suffered stress beyond the call of normal matrimonial duty. Between youth and middle-age she had lost three husbands and innumerable loved ones. She had good cause to shrink from a residential upheaval and life itself. She chose to be a dowager and addressed as the Dowager Countess instead of – more dashingly – Diana Countess of Westmorland. As far as she could she bowed out of the social scene, clove to her children and literally cultivated her garden.

Confidence was likely to have been in short supply. She had made at least two unsatisfactory marriages by private standards. She had reason to believe she was a fool about money. She had got out of the way of consorting with clever amusing people, partly because my father preferred sporting beauty and brawn to brains and could embarrass her socially, and now she did not feel equal to meeting them. The label of goose, teasingly tied round her neck by her siblings, was having effects similar to those of ball and chain.

Rose departed. Nanny was prevailed upon not to leave Lyegrove for the time being. My mother fell into the restorative and peaceful routine of her later life.

In the mornings she organised, wrote letters, did the shopping and swapped gossip with neighbours in Chipping Sodbury, and walked the dogs. She had lunch with Nanny, rested, gardened, and in the early evening went up to the old nursery to be entertained with fond reminiscences and clues of the crossword. After supper she concentrated on her needlework – an example of it was once exhibited in St James's Palace where it won golden opinions. She stitched and listened to the wireless, put out the dogs – a geriatric white peke called Mistletoe or Misty for short, and a mongrel Welsh collie called Angel – and at ten o'clock retired to her bedroom and books.

She had friends in the neighbourhood, but did not see them as often as she might have done because she felt too poor to return their hospitality, and out of practice. She seemed happy enough at Christmas and Easter, when we children returned to occupy our otherwise empty rooms and for a few days all was once more fun and games, and happier still when a grandchild arrived to spend part of the holidays or some member of the family to convalesce after illness: her decision to stay put at Lyegrove looked sensible and unselfish from the point of view of such occasions. But our visits were fleeting, children have to go back to school, and recuperation is by definition finite.

She was strongly attached to Nanny – and as distressed as we were by Nanny's sudden and debilitating blindness.

But – again – time was rushing by, and the longer she had to look after Nanny the more she was persuaded her recent existence had been needlessly quiet and monotonous, and she was burying her talent.

IT WAS WHEN Nanny died that June asked me if I would be spending weekends at Lyegrove in future.

I hope my answer in the affirmative and actions to match it were reassuring.

But forces other than my occasional company were changing Mama's attitudes. Ten years had passed since my father's death: she had recovered so far as possible from the harrowing experiences that led to it. She was sixty-five, already an old age pensioner. She had also weathered more than half a century of emotional storms, and she still felt young and was evidently in the pink of condition. She had proved her fortitude – she and her health had stood up to all the hurtful slings and sharp arrows aimed at them by fortune.

The loss of the daily companionship of Nanny was a blow. Equally not having to wait on and attend to Nanny in her blindness was a relief.

Time was clearing the decks as usual, leaving her on her own: a state of affairs with undoubted appeal to her tidy and independent spirit.

She was supported by her children, although now Rose, as well as Anne, June and David, was married and preoccupied by parenthood: she did not like to ask more of them than that they should keep in touch and come to Lyegrove when inclined.

She probably was or had been urged to re-marry by female if not by male friends. In her fifties she might have wavered and wished for a kind reliable husband to escort her over the horizon and into the sunset. But she had acquired a taste for staying single. She was prepared to pay the price – that is in loneliness – of exercising her right as a Lister to do exactly as she pleased. She preferred freedom and flirtation to commitment, constraint, obligation and potential misery: she was in favour of laughter, having had enough of tears. And she had reached an age that entitled her to ridicule matrimonial propositions.

These late developments hastened or were hastened by her liberation from the influence of Aunt Laura. Own Mummy had been more crushed by the sorrows of life than Own Baby was. The instant death of her husband Lord Lovat at a race-meeting in 1933; then the death of the youngest of her five children in 1940, a daughter in her early teens, also called Rose like my mother's last child; and the anxiety mingled with pride she surely suffered on account of Shimi's wartime heroics and wounds and the clandestine military activities of her other son Hugh, affectionately known as Fearless Fraser – strained her nervous system to breaking-point, setting aside the effects on her heart. She sank into a depression similar to that which seems to have overwhelmed Lord Ribblesdale intermittently, and emerged from protracted medical treatment with her looks gone and her intelligence frayed at the edges.

She was the benefactress of the Scottish Highlands, where she introduced the district nursing scheme; the beauty that once dazzled her contemporaries; the latter-day Egeria of many authors and artists, who gave a home to Maurice Baring in his declining years; a leading light of Roman Catholicism, and the arbiter of taste in houses and gardens. Her power over my mother had been extreme and even supreme by all accounts. But now she was a semi-invalid and not to be taken too seriously.

I got to know her during those fortnights she would spend under her little sister's roof and wing at Lyegrove. She could be irritable and unreasonable. But I loved her pale flexuous long-fingered hands which were still beautiful, her saturnine humour and air of ruined grandeur.

She was a different type from my mother, taller and somewhat heavy-limbed, with a nose that turned up instead of a straight one, and intellectual rather than practical interests. She laid claim to having a more passionate nature. She talked a lot in an authoritative style, laughing and showing her shining white teeth and often getting her facts wrong.

In passing I must admit she was an exception to my cynical rule according to which upper-class status is merely a matter of having money and re-distributing it. After a longish and troublesome visit she would reward my mother's housekeeper – for instance – with a tip to the tune of five shillings or 25p in today's currency. Yet she was treated like a queen, respected and admired by those who served her, and pitied for feeling melancholy and thinking she was poor.

Several other factors helped to bring about the change of climate of my mother's Indian summer. She had found in Victor Hunter the gifted gardener of her dreams, and the same applied to the housekeeper mentioned above, Mrs Gulwell by name. For years Mrs Gulwell had been employed at Lyegrove in various capacities: she was now in command on the domestic front. She and my mother were the firmest friends, and she was an extremely clever, energetic and jolly woman, not a cook by profession but a keen and talented amateur, who greatly improved the standard of food on offer and wanted visitors to come and try it.

My mother, like Aunt Laura, saved her pennies while spending pounds in hopes of keeping the spectre of bankruptcy at bay and putting something aside for her children to inherit. Granted, her financial problems were severe; but their very severity mocked her conscientious attempts to solve them by refraining from the purchase of a second cutlet.

Partly due to Mrs Gulwell's encouragement, or perhaps because she had seen the economic light on the road to Chipping Sodbury, she began to dispense relatively lavish hospitality. Her lunches of meat roasted to a turn and rare old-fashioned puddings like spotted dog, roly-poly with treacle, bread pudding and apple dumplings were sought after, and her teas became a byword. She gave her guests at least as good as she had ever got from them.

I imagine her train of thought was roughly as follows: 'I'm growing old, and ought to let people see what I've made of Lyegrove, and enjoy it. My work's pretty well done, and I wouldn't mind the satisfaction of the odd pat on the back. I've been too busy for friendship: now it's too late to be unfriendly or stand-offish.' Her religion could have contributed the comfortable words: 'The Lord will provide.' And she probably had recourse to the hoary original hymn of emancipation: 'Why not?'

I WOULD GO further and suggest she began to be happier than ever before.

She lowered her defences and risked rather more exposure to the world of others. The success of the experiment was the thin end of a wedge of sorts.

The force of her charms must have conquered hearts and minds from the day she was born. But she had felt overshadowed by Laura, also possibly by Boy Capel's intellect and infidelity and my father's glad-handedness.

Lurking around in her was always a sense of her inadequacy, which combining with her modesty had a repressive effect. She would not have it that she was admirable and did not altogether relish being told she was. Yet now she relaxed and responded to the responses she called forth. She met people at any rate halfway, was less reserved and more tolerant, and made a host of new friends, who came to Lyegrove not only for the food. Soon she was as desirous of company as formerly of solitude.

The irony was that she who had reacted against my father's sociability, and shied away from social intercourse, grew to be more sociable than he had ever been. You could say she had not fancied the sporting fraternity, those re-creations of the characters in Surtees, champion fellows even if they were on the sharp and hot side and sailed a bit near the wind – they knew the score and were good for a laugh. But she formed a specially soft spot for men of that stamp, and giggled at the crackly compliments they paid her over the cucumber sandwiches.

Another ironical thing was her mounting interest in sporting activity and competition. She had coursed greyhounds, hunted to fox-hounds with the best, taught her sons to shoot and taken them shooting – my father was either too nervy to do so or bored by the chore; and she had loved skating and skiing, and a game of anything and better still a match. Yet she had been unenthusiastic to the point of discouragement when it came to her last husband's chief preoccupation.

I suppose she had drawn the line more at the influence than the sportiness of his friends who drank like fishes, shunning any sporting fixture where bars and bookies were to be found. All the same his past and her present passion for sport would have been a bond between them such as they never managed to forge.

A question strikes me: her sporty old age – could it have been a gesture of reparation to my father?

Or was it that without sport on TV she would have died long before she did of the dullness of her existence?

Gallant sportsmen brought over to Lyegrove by David or Rose were a tiny fraction of the mixture of visitors she entertained in her overdue heyday. Aesthetes with an eye for anything pretty, photographers, nobs and knuts, many fellow Roman Catholics, more Protestants, and members of weekend parties in the houses of her local acquaintanceship, came in their curious droves, and eventually gardeners from every corner of the globe, bus-loads of them sometimes, and horticultural million-aires, and horny-handed sons of the soil, amateurs, pro-fessionals and specialists.

She spent hours and hours strolling round and showing off her garden, almost day in and day out from April until October. I cannot believe she was ever much happier than at six o'clock-ish on a lovely summer's evening in the early nineteen-seventies. She would prolong her tea party, waiting for the sun to sink behind the grove of trees and cease to glare at her flowers, then suggest: 'Shall we go out? Would you like to see the garden?' And calling her dog or dogs, often in vain, for the dogs unlike their mistress were soon bored to distraction by the same circumambient tour, and donning a head-scarf and light-ing another cigarette against the midges she would lead the way onto the terrace and down the steps between the great pillars.

In the end her tolerance amounted to almost indiscriminate friendliness. But age never compromised her power of differentiating good from bad behaviour. She had a special set of criteria by which she judged visitors to her garden even as they were judging it. She expected polite appreciation, but was always pleasantly surprised by praise. She was put out by people who would not concentrate on what they were seeing, but gassed on about trivial matters such as the fate of the nation. She hated those who hustled and bustled round, and the other sort who sat on shooting-sticks studying every single bloom for half an hour.

'So-and-so's a menace,' she would say: 'she kept me standing by her wheelchair while she gawped at flowers until I could have killed her willingly.'

Perhaps her main objection to persons who rushed or dawdled was that they might not register the full impact of her combinations of colours, and would miss the point it had taken her fifty years to make.

THE BRAININESS OF some of her new friends was a particular satisfaction and delight. As explained above her breeding and upbringing should have inclined her to feel at home in the company of the brainiest people, but in her middle years she had steered clear of them.

A beneficial side-effect of the ageing process was that she no longer minded making a fool of herself – and incidentally and consequently never did. She could not be bothered with snobbery of the inverted intellectual or any other kind. She had ceased to be a respecter of persons – I mean in the courteous sense of that idiom. While she loved her old faithfuls as much as ever, she was excited to excite clever strangers, especially clever men of the world, with her historical relationships and memories, her distinction, the romance of her habitat, and her geniality.

In the mid-sixties Aunt Laura had died. My mother must have expected her death: so far as I can remember she took it remarkably calmly considering the lifelong closeness of their sisterhood. Of course age wastes less time mourning its dead than youth; and now she had no one to feel inferior to.

She played the part of merry widow with increasing zest – and never seemed too old for it. Tea was her favourite meal. She had a digestion as strong as my father's was weak, and always a hearty appetite for bread and jam, let alone treats for parties like bun-rings and lardy cakes.

Sitting at the head of the refectory table with a tray of teacups and the flat silver teapot in front of her, she addressed her guests as opportunity offered. She wished conversation to be general, but her manners were too good to silence anyone who tried to talk only to his or her neighbour. She was embarrassed by pretentious remarks and would rather have died than make one. She would if she could avoid the conversational quicksand of culture. She was bored by controversy and detested strife.

Her subject in a word was herself. Yet she was less egocentric than most of us: her social aim was to please and amuse. She complained funnily and had a gift for self-mockery, and never fell into the trap crammed with senior citizens of forgetting wit is brief.

She distilled laughter from the treatment meted out to her by her staff. She was tickled by the encouraging greeting she received from a cleaning woman twice a week: 'Oh milady, you look awful – are you feeling all right?' Once her application for a driving licence was turned down: she had signed the form filled in by my father's old chauffeur, who had answered in the affirmative the question of whether or not she was epileptic. She giggled infectiously at her recollection of the time she had gone somewhere for tea, said goodbye and left the house after dark, got in her car and waited for the above-mentioned chauffeur to emerge from the domestic department and drive her home: he sauntered out and, not seeing her, imagining he was alone, relieved himself against the car's front wheel.

She loved the story recounted by her gardener Victor Hunter, a strongly-built grizzled rustic, of the visitor to Lyegrove who encountered him in the shadowy kitchen passage and called: 'Hullo, Diana!'

She dined out on her confession that in a fit of absent-mindedness at a nephew's wedding she had instructed the majordomo to announce her as the bridegroom's niece instead of his aunt; and on the saga of her collision with a van delivering Mother's Pride bread. The delivery-man had hauled her up into his cab to discuss the accident, and was so handsome and charming she was quite sure he must indeed be the pride of his mother.

She was at her best when being egged on and teased by a member of the opposite sex as flirtatious as she was. But she was seldom at a complete loss for something to say. Her father had dinned into his children the lesson that in company they were to speak at all costs: rightly in my opinion he considered silence to be amongst the most heinous of the crimes selfishness commits against polite society.

Luckily she never grew out of her faculty to giggle and lose control. The funnier thing about the wedding at which she in her eighties was proclaimed to be the niece of the bridegroom in his twenties was that she was so paralysed by laughing at the mistake that she halted the whole procession of guests. Her irrepressible laughter, the undimmed glow of her complexion, and taking more interest in the present than the past, were vital constituents of the impression of youthfulness she could still create.

One day a child was asked what she had thought of the antiquated lady she had just met, namely my mother.

'Well – I didn't think she was old,' the little girl replied.

'I wonder why not?'

The reason given was mysterious: 'Because she smoked a cigarette and how she smoked it.'

AT THIS HAPPY time, which she had spent so long waiting for and earned the hard way in an emotional sense, June and I stayed with her alternately and at intervals, and David had his home not far off, and Rose lived two miles down the road: Anne who had emigrated to Spain was the only one of her children she did not see regularly. As for her eleven grandchildren, she received them in relays.

A weekend at Lyegrove had suffered a sea-change. Comparatively speaking, it had become a social extravaganza. We visited and entertained visitors to meals, and family reunions filled every other spare minute.

Oscar Wilde observed that we judge our parents and sometimes forgive them. When I assumed a certain responsibility for my mother I had already forgiven and began to appreciate her. She had brought us up admirably, not shifting too much of the burden of her marital cares onto our shoulders, not circumscribing our freedom to roam the countryside or bicycle on the roads or shoot or dare to do dangerous things, not fussing over and never spoiling us: apart from shooting, which was my particular pleasure, the great treats of my childhood were the pantomime in Bristol, the afternoon of the Mop or annual fair in Chipping Sodbury, and expeditions every fortnight or so to Bath – riding ponies was a mixed blessing in my experience and often more like a curse. She had exerted an effortless discipline which did not oppress, entered into our victories and defeats and nursed us through our illnesses with expertise and devotion. I acknowledged my gratitude and grew fonder of her. But cool and reserved remain the adjectives applicable to our relations, affectionate as they were.

I like to think the form or formality of our relationship suited her. She had a man not exactly around the house – she had sampled constant masculine company and could not abide it – but coming to Lyegrove for a couple of nights every twenty-one days and doing the dirtier work of running the place, on call between times if need be, whose efforts to preserve his own independence were protective of hers, and for whom the object of the exercise was to pay his debts and simply to please rather than to be pleased or put her under any sort of obligation.

Her widowhood had not been trouble-free. Anne's and Rose's divorces, and then the death of June's first husband, were causes of distress. She was more and more worried by recurrent and deepening financial crises. Her failing eyesight, and a disease that affects hands, as a result of which six of her fingers had contracted and were immobilised, no longer permitted her to do her needlework.

Yet she seemed to have accumulated a philosophic store, a store of stoicism, which even the greedy depredations of fate would never exhaust.

Of course she had much to be thankful for and – at last – made happy by. Her health was still positively rude: those years of considering herself and being considered delicate, of early to bed and not so early to rise, and general moderation and a routine as regular as that of her dogs, may have been responsible, although statistics would probably prove her robust longevity was just a matter of luck. She had energy and stamina, clarity of mind, perfect memory, and modernity of outlook owing to her exclusive interest in the here and now. And she was more stimulated than tired by social activity.

She had won a measure of renown by making a home and a garden – in other words by doing what came naturally. It must have given her confidence to realise she had survived the assaults of destiny: which, therefore, had perhaps tempered the metal of her being.

She loved her descendants, not least for loving her. If I was a bit like the bread and butter of her existence, June, David and Rose were the jam. She was closer to June than to any of us, she kept no secrets from June and vice versa. She was excited by David's achievements and amused by his jokes. Her feelings for Rose were a longer story. Suffice it to say for the moment that she was traditionally anxious about the welfare of the youngest of her children, saddened by Rose's second marriage, and glad they were getting on so well and seeing so much of each other – Rose came to tea with her almost every day, often bringing friends along, and fetched and carried, organised jaunts and excursions, and was the main source of her fun.

Ever more fulfilled by living, unwilling to leave the party of life although ready to die if she had to, comforted by religion anyway, aristocratic yet not stuck up, not intellectual yet brilliantly intuitive, she was an object lesson in the art of growing old with grace, and nearly the mindless sage we sometimes called her, that paradoxical description of the ideal aspired to by Zen Buddhism.

The roughest and smoothest occurrences of her eighty-fourth year, or rather the smoothest and roughest in that order, were that I married and Rose contracted cancer.

I WAS AFRAID my wife Gillian would find the rigours of winter at Lyegrove – and autumn and spring – intolerable; and my mother shared my fears and regretfully suggested that in future I should only come down and bring her to stay in summer.

The central heating system was installed in the 1920s. It had gone wrong and been switched off some ten years previously – not that its disuse made much difference in the context, since there were no radiators in the bedroom we would have to sleep in, and indeed not many elsewhere.

That bedroom at a corner of the house had three large windows plus open fireplace and chimney, and was phenomenally cold and damp for between seven and nine months of the year. It boasted a power-plug for an electric heater. But I was loth to run up my mother's electricity bills and – more so – to put the slightest additional strain on wires and cables also dating back to the twenties. Bitter experience warned me that if I should yield to the temptation to try to be a little warmer, one of the hundred or so fuses in various cupboards and outhouses would blow and require me to spend hours and days looking for it; while my imagination summoned colourful pictures of an electric spark setting fire to the place and incinerating the inmates.

The bathroom that would be ours was another big room, facing north and not warm even in midsummer.

Downstairs my mother had by now chosen to live in the front-cum-dining-hall with the television set: which had the front door opening into it, two more doors, also a swing-door to the back parts of the house, again three large windows, the staircase at one end leading to extensive landings and passages, and a floor of oak boards with gaps in between through which draughts clammy or cutting or both rose from the cellar. She would spend winter's evenings sitting at the head of the table, turning her chair one way to eat her tea and chat, another to watch TV programmes: we traipsed into the kitchen for supper. The Pither stove, burning solid fuel, threw out some heat, and the central rug on the floor put a partial stopper on the vertical draughts. But to sit farther from the stove than my mother did, at any rate until you were used to the conditions, was to congeal and freeze, however many clothes you had on.

The discomforts of Lyegrove were not confined to the temperature or any particular season. The hot water boiler was like a spoilt pet which cannot be relied upon to behave itself when strangers come to the house. Invariably it refused to function at Christmas and would keep me down in the cellar coaxing and cajoling it for the best part of the festivities.

And rain had no difficulty in getting through not merely

the roof, but the two storeys below, notwithstanding the plethora of buckets and bowls in the attic. My flesh creeps at the recollection of frantic days and nights of baling out during storms; and the dread of sounds indicative of the house having sprung a leak; and the hope as I drifted towards sleep of not being woken by water dripping onto the bed; and the horrid sensation of walking over carpet that squelched underfoot although meant to be dry.

But Gilly put up with it all. She forgave Lyegrove its every defect for the sake of its qualities. She thought the summer there was worth the price of the winter – actually not too steep a price by her reckoning, since she would expatiate on the additional scenic charms of snow and frost even as I was feeling queasy about their effect on the fabric of the building.

Moreover she immediately loved and was loved by her mother-in-law. Gilly's admiration, appreciation and sympathy were amongst the compensations of my mother's last years. But they could not stop the rising tide of her sorrow in respect of Rose.

HER OTHER CHILDREN and her grandchildren had at times been seriously ill.

But Rose was different – and not only in partisan maternal opinion.

She was in her mid-forties, twice married, and the mother of three, when the trouble began. She was very young for her years, still childlike in some respects. She had no intellectual interests to speak of; hardly ever read a book – it took her years to wade through one; was blissfully ignorant of the topics of the day; and self-absorbed in that she was not above giving in to her moods and moodiness. She had taken against her mother when she was a girl, making no secret of her inexplicable and wounding antipathy; then round about the age of thirty she swung towards the opposite extreme, developing a filial dependency that was almost onerous. She had always been a storm centre in the family meteorology. And she continued to be exceptionally nervous where health or ill-health was concerned: Nanny used to beg us not to mention any disease in Rose's hearing because she would be bound to imagine she had it and play up accordingly.

At the same time, unexpectedly maybe, considering she was a centre not only of storms but also therefore of attention, she had a completely unspoilt side, a fresh approach to life, and poignant air of wonder again of a child.

She loved activity, excitement, drama, and crises capable of resolution by means of her energy and resourcefulness. She loved a challenge, an outing, holiday, treat, playing a game or watching one, any sporting occasion. Her spiritual home was a social gathering – she had a gift for getting the party spirit and making a party go: it seemed to be her vocation to chat to people. Although academically dim or more likely lazy, and a bit of a Mrs Malaprop into the bargain – she could talk about an experience that went to somebody's head like water – her responsiveness and humour were clever. An egoist from one point of view, from another she was altruistic in her readiness to encourage and console friends in difficulty, and provide support.

She was better at friendship than love: that is more successful. The booby-trap for women she stumbled into was that she attracted and was attracted to an overtly masculine type she could not manage – she was too vulnerable and complex, and lacked the sensuality and earthiness which might have compensated for emotional incompatibility. Perhaps her ideal partner never did exist: to be at once dominant and amenable, faithful to and forgiving of an incorrigible flirt, sensitive and yet unmoved by gloom and despondency, fond and yet not particularly physical, amused by folly, and able to pay for the sorts of entertainment supposed to palliate restlessness, is a tall order.

She dedicated herself to the task of parenthood – she was more enthusiastic as mother than as wife. But it could be that she tried too hard to please her children, especially after her divorce from their father, and more especially when she introduced a step-father into their lives.

Whatever her faults, surely more or less minor, she had that quality which defeats analysis – she was lovable. Good sisters and good friends, loyal and dutiful, never quarrelsome or grasping, such as Rose was, may be nothing to write home about. The difference in her was the talent for touching hearts.

Her divorce in her thirties was a miserable business for everyone mixed up in it. The torment for my mother was having to sit on the side-lines, powerless to protect her baby. And then Rose's failure to find happiness at her second matrimonial attempt was rendered no easier to bear by the fact that they were both ten years older.

But her illness was worse. Striking so defenceless a person when she was down seemed to all who cared for her exceptionally cruel, even judging by fate's standards of cruelty.

SHE RECOVERED, SHE recovered repeatedly from the courses of treatment and surgical operations she had to undergo, and half-accepted the reasons she was given to account for her condition.

Mama insisted that Rose's nerves and innate paranoia in respect of illness would never stand the truth. Perhaps her inclination to keep off so disagreeable a subject was partly old-fashioned. But no one knowing and loving Rose wanted to take the risk of making things more difficult for her.

I hope our lies were white and right, even if they tied the hands of her medical advisers to some extent, and were apt to cause uncertainty which is not much good as medicament.

The main repository of the fears inspired by her strange symptoms and their remedial consequences was Mama. Rose's children and friends did all they could to calm and comfort her; but her reflex action was to telephone or return to Lyegrove for reassurance. And the prompt intensity of Mama's sympathetic responses was remarkable in an octogenarian. Whether or not she derived any satisfaction from the evidence of being needed, she was often exhausted by as many as half a dozen telephone calls and a couple of tearful visits in a single day. Not that she grudged the effort – she would have died on the spot in order that her daughter might be spared – she would have done anything to right the wrong of Rose being relatively young and ailing whereas she was old and strong. At least her attitude to ill-health again and again proved its worth. Her medical knowledge may have been out of date, although she had maintained her interest in medicine; her nice mixture of trust in doctors, scepticism, refusal to be blinded by science, insights, patience and show of confidence were nonetheless a sort of tonic. She had a way of greeting bad news by saying: 'How boring . . . How boring for you,' which somehow put diseases in their place.

I remember arriving at Lyegrove on a Friday afternoon to stay for the weekend, and Rose joining us as usual for tea, the bang of the back door, her quick light step in the passage, her entry into the front hall where I met her, and her announcement that she had noticed another peculiar lump on the side of her face while driving over. I cannot forget her shocked looks and the dread in her voice. We told Mama, who said: 'It's a swollen gland – you've probably picked up a bug that's lodged there – we'll go to the doctor and get it seen to – poor darling, what a bore!' No doubt Rose had jumped to a more ominous conclusion, as I had. But Mama, notwithstanding her awareness of the physical damage the lump might be doing and the emotional damage it had already done, would neither anticipate events nor yield to pessimism, apprehensive and pessimistic as she was naturally and when she was not under pressure to exercise self-control. Her steadiness had a steadying effect on Rose. We sat down and tried to talk of other things.

And Rose replied to questions about her family and her activities and gradually grew more animated, describing the interior decoration of some house, for instance, or what she had worn or would wear at a party in the past or future. Mama drew her out, laughing at her funny phraseology and inaccuracies, and I did my best to join in. My sister's expression was no longer unsuitably sombre, and her cheeks regained a little colour.

She was never the beauty Mama had been and for that matter remained. But she had one exquisite facial feature, namely her small straight nose, of which words can give no impression; and her appearance was refined continually by her vicissitudes. In middle age she had not lost her slim athletic figure. She was mad about tennis – and not allowed to play by her illness. Disappointment was her daily bread. Disappointment and dread were like the grit in the shell of the oyster that makes the pearl. The shallowness of her sweet frivolity became nobly deep. On that afternoon at Lyegrove she cast aside anguish to try to amuse and not to upset us – likewise Mama for her daughter's sake. The latter was the one with the lump on her face – it had to be cut out later on; but the former would have suffered vicariously the pain of it in full. Rose was letting us have a preview of the heroism which – in a superior sense – was to wrest the ultimate victory from her enemy and killjoy, and Mama was once more living up to her father's dictum that she was the bravest of all.

People sometimes pitied her for not being permitted to have a peaceful old age after the sorrows and the strains. I think on the contrary that Rose and she kept each other going for many years – more years than they would have had separately or we as a family would have had together.

MY MOTHER WAS good at keeping her dogs alive, too. Mistletoe called Misty, the white peke, was nineteen when she died with assistance from the vet. One of the grandchildren multiplied Misty's age by seven to arrive at the supposed human equivalent and would startle strangers by telling them she was a hundred and thirty-three. Angel, the mongrel collie, and Fatty and Lucy, more pekes, were centenarians by the same rule.

Dogs without any routine are like persons out of a job, or at worst prisoners confused and unnerved by the odd hours they are compelled to keep. My mother's knew exactly what they were meant to be doing at virtually every moment of the day: they got their two meals on the dot, queued up to share her piece of plain chocolate at ten-thirty, were taken for their constitutional through the garden and down the drive and back again when she returned from shopping in Chipping Sodbury, rested as she did after lunch, and so on – they were assigned their duties and proud to attend to them. Their health along with hers undoubtedly benefited from the regularity of her habits, and from the extremism of her moderation.

Needless to say she ministered to canine invalids and hypochondriacs with skill and imagination. Once Lucy hurt her paw and had to have it bandaged. Then Lucy's sister Fatty refused food and began to drag herself round the house with a drooping tail. My mother's diagnosis was jealousy: she bandaged up one of Fatty's uninjured paws and wrought an instant cure.

But while she concentrated as it were on life and maintaining it, the rate of deterioration of the fabric of her home – and literally the roof over her head – gathered speed. No patch or running repair could now waterproof the hills and valleys, the dells and wells and gulleys, and the hatches and skylights of the Lyegrove roof. And the costs of renewal of any one of the large component parts, let alone the whole, were prohibitive and beyond her means.

The attic floor with its seven bedrooms and huge box-room had become a kind of no-go area. More often than I would have liked I had to rush up there nonetheless to empty the brimming bowls and buckets. The architect and builders responsible for the work done to the house in the 1920s had two serious crimes to answer for. They had left intact a sizeable space under the eaves, traditionally called the snow-box, the sole purpose of which seemed to be to catch snowflakes and melt them, so that water percolated into the rooms below. And they had sited the hot water tank beside the boiler in that part of the cellar reached by a stone staircase in the courtyard, that is to say in the open air, which cooled it.

The situation out of doors had not been improved by

the passage of the thirty-odd years since it had depressed my father. Undergrowth had encroached on the lower reaches of the front drive, which was almost impassable. And in the garden, where Victor was in charge of the flowers exclusively, bracken and even saplings sprouted from the Georgian summerhouse, and the greenhouses were a pathetic muddle of broken glass, warped wood and giant nettles.

At this time it became clear that for me to pay bills on my mother's behalf was easier than having to cope with crises because she had either lost them or issued cheques for the wrong amount. The more I did to help her the more I was impressed by what she had done: for she had performed with a minimum of fuss all the tasks I was now finding tricky and irksome, and ruled her little empire so efficiently as to create a haven of peace for her offspring and other visitors. And she had done it on a shoestring. I was alarmed as well as impressed by the shortage of available cash. Even forking out for comparatively minor expenses like a burst water-main or a new cesspit for one of the cottages forced me to make actuarial calculations, dividing her resources by the number of years she was likely to survive.

When she had yet another accident in her car, the most damaging effects of which were financial, I suggested she should stop driving. She had been a menace on the roads for some years. She could not see well enough, or manage the controls with her crippled hands. Apparently in the neighbourhood, because she happened to be short-waisted and nowadays slumped down in her seat, so that she had to peer through the steering-wheel, she was known as the headless driver: a joke she appreciated.

She replied: 'Yes, I agree, I must – I can't do it any more – and I'd hate to hurt somebody.'

However unwise she may have been matrimonially and to live at Lyegrove, she had a streak of soundest common sense, setting aside the morality and generosity of her renunciation as it were of her freedom of independent travel. She was a more reliable guide to political opinion countrywide than any pollster. Her inevitable errors of judgment in her old age were not too serious, and often her decisions were vindicated by time and what she began ended better than anyone expected. In her eighty-fifth year her pekes Lucy and Fatty died and she went and bought another, called Sing. Dog-loving outsiders shook their heads over her selfish action. But Sing not only alleviated her loneliness and was the agent of much joy, he also led a perfectly secure, happy and long life.

MY MOTHER FLOURISHED in the lower depths to which the temperature could sink in the front hall at Lyegrove, thin as she was, and although her habitual garb included a V-necked jersey and sandals. She had been brought up in Yorkshire and probably to expect to be cold in winter. But she may not have been as cold as we were. She sat almost on top of the Pither stove and had a rug to wrap round her knees. I remember wondering by about nine o'clock on a Friday evening, having been in the house for a few hours, if I would ever get warm again. Actually by noon on Saturday I had adjusted to the harsh climate in which she chose to live; and other members of the family agreed that time rendered it more bearable. Nevertheless we all tried to move her back into her sitting-room.

She would not hear of it. The smoking-room where we had sat before the war had lining-paper billowing from the walls and ceiling and sagging shutters, and the drawing-room was an empty cavern, its fine furniture sold and its curtains in tatters – she was not going to have her last beautiful room disfigured by a television set: that was the truth of the matter, though she made various excuses.

During an especially bitter spell of weather, when even she was threatened by her doctor with hypothermia, we bought her new electric heaters and begged her to let us pay her electricity bills for ever. Still she dug in her toes, those obstinate toes, that cloven hoof of obstinacy, which had enabled her not to be pulled or pushed from her home. She said she was touched and grateful. But she preferred not to cost us any more than she already did in one way and another. She soon banished the heaters to the cubby-hole under the front stairs, or, ironically, though I hope not consciously so, had them put in our bedrooms to keep us warmer when we visited her.

She had either the obstinate strength of the weak or the weakness of obstinacy of the strong, I could never say which. She was a confusing mixture of undeviating determination and flightiness and whimsicality.

For example a nice small house was to let in Badminton.

We pleaded with her to move there. Out of the question, she replied. The house was not nice, it was jerrybuilt and tumbledown with dark rooms and stairs like a hen-ladder, and cramped and poky rather than small. Besides it would break her old heart to leave Lyegrove. Did we want to break her heart?

Friends of hers rented the house, did it up and invited her to come and inspect the finished article. She returned to sing its praises. It was delightful, pretty as a picture, cosy and convenient with its rooms the right size, modern heating which was dirt-cheap to run, labour-saving machines and tailored kitchen, and just a stone's throw from the village shops. It would have suited her to a T. She was afraid a golden opportunity had been missed. Why had we failed to draw her attention to it?

We reminded her of our pleas. Knowing the excellence of her memory we remonstrated with her for forgetting. She apologised and giggled.

She could carry her occasional inability to see herself as others saw her to whimsical lengths. The funniest aspect of her attachment to Lyegrove was her signal lack of sympathy for anyone else feeling and doing the same sort of thing. She would berate two of her dearest friends – sisters – for staying on in the house with a mere four bedrooms in which they had lived with their mother.

'They can't afford it,' she explained to us. 'They're absurdly over-housed. They're so sentimental – I laughed at them for ruining themselves for silly sentimental reasons. They should sell their home immediately instead of rattling about in it, and buy a tiny practical cottage somewhere, which is all they need.'

[ 123 ]

LYEGROVE IN MIDWINTER left a deep impression not only on the members of my mother's family. It shattered the illusions of many a stranger invited to tea, foreigners especially, Americans, grandees from the continent. Information had probably reached American ears in respect of the high-born old lady living in a charming house in an enchanted garden at the back of beyond. Aristocratic persons from France – say – would be likely to know her lineage and matrimonial record. Such visitors for the first time expected to find her in circumstances and surroundings befitting her reputation and station.

I think of them pityingly at half-past four o'clock on a wet and windy afternoon in December or January. They were often tempted to turn off the main road into the front drive by the stone gate-posts and gothic lodge. The potholes tested the springs of cars, the rampant undergrowth scratched paintwork, not to mention the hazard of fallen and falling trees. If or when they reached the halfway mark, they would come up against a five-barred gate, closed years ago to prevent our dogs getting out and others getting in, anchored in muddy compost, impossibly heavy and liable to disintegrate at a touch.

With luck they chose the back drive and stopped by the entrance to the courtyard in which the back door might be found. But then, if they were polite or simply puzzled, they were inclined to make the mistake of looking for the door at the front of the house, which meant opening rusty wrought-iron gates, negotiating steps, and going round by the terrace of uneven slippery flagstones interspersed with plants and flowerbeds all too easy to trip over in the dark.

On the other hand, if they succeeded in blundering into the courtyard they would have to decide which of the eight doors therein led to house and hostess, meanwhile avoiding the pitfall of the central stairway descending to the cellar and boiler-room. And the right door had no bell or flap for letters to distinguish it from the others.

The tough tradition was that you plumped for it, barged in, switched on lights, braved barking dogs, and via the grubby passage serving kitchen, backstairs, pantry, cloakroom, arrived at and pushed through the swing-door – which swung no longer – into the front hall.

Supposing the stranger paying a visit was not alone but had been brought by some knowledgeable intermediary, and was therefore neither begrimed by struggling with the gate in the front drive, nor unnerved by narrow squeaks in the courtyard where once a tipsy odd-job man tumbled down the steps and broke his neck, he or she would receive an enthusiastic welcome: the welcome was perhaps adequate compensation for the potential difficult-ies and dangers of winning through to it. My mother loved a new face, she never ceased to make new friends, and was capable of showing her hospitable pleasure in a delightfully demonstrative fashion. She embraced anyone who gave her a chance. Shaking hands she would explain that the contraction of her fingers used to be called Coachman's Disease, because a coachman held reins, as she had in her horsey young days: but she put the blame on her needlework. She would dazzle with her smiles, and thank people for coming, and apologise somewhat complacently for the obstacles, and ask questions and show interest and make them feel at home. And the teas she provided would sharpen the most sated of appetites: sandwiches not only of cucumber, also of lettuce and Marmite, one of Mrs Gulwell's specialities, and the bread she took trouble to get, fresh from the bakery, and strawberry jam, and the sponge cakes dusted with icing sugar and layered with a scrumptious filling.

Yet feminine eyes at any rate, however beguiled by her beauty and so on, must have remarked the threadbare state of her cardigan: for years she clung on to a favourite green cardigan that came to look as if it had been knitted by spiders. She had once been noted for the smartness of her clothes and way of wearing them. Nowadays, while always dressing in good taste and neatly, she prided herself on not paying undue attention to appearances – and would argue in an attempt to justify the extravagance of Lyegrove and her garden that she spent scarcely a penny on personal adornment.

Moreover she so loved a bargain that – for example – she allowed no one to ignore the cheap and nasty handbag she used. She would show it round and boast of its having cost her next to nothing. Thus she astonished certain American millionairesses and French dukes, and snobs from every country, who probably felt she was carrying

English eccentricity rather far and letting the side down.

But their astonishment was not yet complete. Those visitors belonging to a large-ish party who sat at the wrong end of the refectory table, that is to say at a greater distance from the Pither stove, congealed almost visibly. Icy blasts in the form of draughts from every direction buffeted them. The higher the wind the worse it was; and high winds, the curse of the place in its relatively altitudinous location, were productive of another disagreeable effect in the dining-hall. They would squeeze past the sprung copper strip that edged the front door in a vain attempt to draught-proof it and intermittently cause a loud twang and fearful vibratory moaning.

WINTER VISITORS, COMING and going in the dark, and seeing nothing of Lyegrove except the front hall and kitchen passage – the sitting-room was usually too cold for a nose to be poked into – were to know neither the reasonable origins of my mother's way of life in her latter days, nor the attractive qualities of her home. No doubt, and at least, they wondered what all the fuss was about. They did not realise that by freezing indoors they were making a kind of negative contribution to the cause of money saved for spending outdoors. They were ignorant of summer's answers to their queries.

And they were not exactly helped by my mother, who, as disablement crept up on her and denied her the handicrafts and other ploys that had occupied house-bound evenings, hated winter more and more and regarded it as just marking time.

But spring occurred early in her calendar. She passed on to me her fetish in respect of the shortest day of the year, when spring seemed to her almost to start, and the longest, the twenty-first of June, after which summer seemed prematurely autumnal. She looked forward to the twenty-first of December, and gloated over each extra minute of daylight like a miser counting additions to his hoard of gold. At Christmas she loved to find the green shoots of snowdrops pushing through moss in the grove and under the trees in the drive. She chose to take them as promises that the worst was over.

Nature rudely declined to fulfil her hopes. I mean to say that more often than not her so-called spring was the harbinger of disappointment – which she never learned to expect. She would almost forgive snow, for it could turn out to have been the gardener's friend, protective and chemically beneficial, notwithstanding its bad habit of breaking down clipped yew hedges. But frost and a blighting easterly wind were beyond the pale of horticultural toleration. She agonised as her plants perished either in reality or in her imagination. When the battle with the weather allowed she would sadly count the casualties – and then brace herself to play the lead in that annual drama of suspense, the subject of which was getting the grass of her lawns mown at the right time. She could be too early – her temperamental lawnmower broke down if the grass was very short – or too late – her lawnmower would have nothing to do with taller stronger grass. The strain of such decisions made her ill temporarily in her old age.

It was not irrational of her to worry. The English climate can skip spring altogether, boiling and burning where it froze the day before, and transforming lawns into hayfields.

Summer in March, whatever the effect it had on the herbage of Lyegrove, offered an explanation of some of my mother's hibernatory habits.

Every door was immediately thrown open. All day long the circling sun shone on the southern front of the house. It streamed through the doorway and windows into the front hall, dewy and sparkling in the morning, already filled with gnats and midges in the afternoon. The condensation dried on the walls of the rooms that had been shut up, and in the evening the roseate light of sunset, filtered by the trees of the grove, skeletal and gently swaying, permeated the west-facing sitting-room with brilliant flickers.

In the hot weather of some exceptional spring that proved its chilly rule, or in summer, everybody's inclination was to come in and collapse on the nearest chairs – those round the refectory table in the front hall – before going out again: which was probably the real and rather touching reason why my mother sat there in winter, because she was as close as possible and poised to return to her garden. She was proud to show people her sitting-room and entertain there when the temperature permitted. She opened the house and garden to the public twice a year, for nurses and for her church, and would fill the drawing-room with so many vases of flowers that the absence of furniture was scarcely noticeable. Again she was proud of the proportions of the drawing-room, and the greenish colour she had painted it, and the carved pine mantelpiece seven feet high complete with heraldic devices. But she was always happiest in the front hall. She dozed in its only comfortable chair after lunch instead of retiring to a room in which she would have been less likely to be disturbed.

Summer visitors could see the point at once of her preference and of having had to come in by the back door. After the shades of the cramped kitchen passage they were surprised by the space of the hall suffused with sunlight and fragrant airiness, and by the view through the wide open door of the receding greensward of the former front drive. The dogs whose escapism had caused her to close the gate halfway down were no more; but she had kept the gate closed and continued to ban cars. She loved the sort of lawn a hundred yards long which the drive had become, edged by rougher grass where the seasonal wild flowers grew beneath the sweeping green branches of beech trees. She had mourned the fact that her garden was not immediately in front of the house: the vista and perspective of that verdant promenade reaching right from the front door into the woodland haze of the middle distance was the next best thing.

SHE WOULD ESCORT her visitors towards the garden, say at the time both of the day and the year that most flattered it, early evening in mid-June.

[ 130 ]

A trunk road was just visible and audible from certain vantage points at Lyegrove; and there was the main road at the bottom of the drive. Yet by common consent it was an extraordinarily peaceful place – it seemed to be situated in the deepest country, far from the cares and crazier preoccupations of the great world. This impression was fostered by the walls and hedges, both about ten feet tall, enclosing the pair of linked gardens. The lowing of cows and bark of a dog across at the farm, the vocalising of rooks, jackdaws and wood-pigeons, or song of a blackbird standing at ease on a manorial ball crowning one of the pillars – such sounds accompanied by the ceaseless humming of insects accentuated the quietness.

Amongst my mother's gifts of horticultural showmanship was her strong-minded refusal to regret decisions she had taken or carp at work done – at least publicly. And she was a typical gardener in that she saw no reason to be modest about the virtues of her flowers. She would boast of their beauty and delightful habits, and with the aid of her walking-stick draw attention to the harmony of their juxtaposed colours.

Eyes sharper than hers had become, and more expert than mine, might have detected novel signs of soft-heartedness in the pruning and a consequential disorder in the exuberant greenery. On the other hand the incipient relaxation of control added a sort of naturalism to the formalised scene, as if the garden had at last given its keepers the slip and was growing in such artful profusion simply for the pleasure of doing so.

After the tour had lasted for about an hour she would suggest a little rest on the seat above the sunken lily pool.

Swallows and martins circled and dipped to drink the water in the pool, fluttering upwards amidst a shower of diamond and ruby droplets caught in the rays of the setting sun. The steps leading to various levels were dreamily uneven and the lichened flagstones of paths and paved areas were outlined by flowers. Even candid friends had to admit the garden was still marvellous, and as its spokeswoman she would make her annual claim that it was better than ever.

I remember sitting between my wife and my mother on that seat, while the latter in expansive and unwonted mood, smoking to keep off the midges, reminisced. She would tell tales, for instance, of the ruthless womanising of Prime Minister Asquith, married to her aunt Margot, Charty Ribblesdale's sister; or the occasion when she bravely left a luncheon table and dining-room because her fellow-guest and old friend Winston Churchill had such abominable manners and refused to speak to her; or John Sargent's sole utterance while he was doing her portrait in charcoal, 'You've got jolly hair.'

Perhaps she lingered in the garden because she realised it had reached a peak of perfection and could only go downhill. Perhaps, again, she wanted everyone to make the most of her half century of creative labour, knowing that gardens are an extension of the personality of the gardener and when she was dead hers would die, sadly enough in spite of her belief in resurrection. Certainly she postponed the stroll indoors if possible, since at her age she could not be sure she would have another chance to stroll out.

But fulfilment, not fear, was the social keynote she

struck. These days the distinctive feature of her dealings with people was confidence. And in private she even remained confident of Rose's cure.

Her summer visitors had a nice time with the help of the weather. Although they were forced to arrive and depart by the tradesmen's entrance, they were surely susceptible to the spells woven by their hostess and her habitation, which were the opposite of disappointing.

GOOD GARDENERS ARE rare; good gardeners with good taste, like Victor Hunter, are rarer.

But Victor too was growing old. He no longer had the energy to prune as severely as he used to or clip yew hedges. And now he and my mother arrived at various uncharacteristic decisions which satisfied the need to save labour only at the expense of the general scenic scheme. Flowerbeds were picked apparently at random to be grassed over. A rubbish-dump was established at close quarters to the house and one of the main garden gates: when lit, it smouldered and belched evil-smelling smoke for weeks on end. Pretty weeds such as valerian were permitted to ramp all over the place.

Then Victor's health gave out. He had to retire, and his son Keith could not manage the garden single-handed.

And my mother fell and broke her wrist, and on another occasion fell and broke her pelvis, and little by little her constitution had to yield to the onset of the passing years.

She suffered spells in hospital, where she was apt to contract the extra ailment of homesickness. Her legs began to fail her, and her eyesight, and her appetite, and eventually her zest for living.

Not these commonplace developments, but the reactions of individuals to them, are sometimes interesting.

My mother said: 'If I had two new feet I'd be okay,' and: 'If you cut off my head and transplanted it onto a better body than mine, I'd have no complaints.'

She said old age was different from most other illnesses because there was no chance of a cure for it.

She flirted and fell in love with her doctors, who often seemed to reciprocate her feelings. She shocked new ones with accounts of the variety of pills she took, and mocked them for telling her the barbiturates that had helped her to sleep since the year dot were bad for the nonagenarian she nearly was. She had a metabolism that responded favourably to drugs and anaesthetics – they caused her virtually no hangover. The less active she became the more cigarettes she was pleased to smoke.

Her inability to see herself as others saw her had its uses. A clever and cruel programme about old age was shown on TV. I hoped she had not watched it. I was afraid she would have been hurt and depressed by the ridicule disguised as compassion it heaped on persons in her situation. But she enjoyed it thoroughly and was tickled by the peccadillos of the participants which were similar to her own.

Her sense of humour stood her in good stead. We applied to one of the agencies which supply women on a fortnightly basis to help those disabled by age or for other reasons. Three arrived in succession: the first was a compulsive eater and looked it – she must have weighed twenty stone; the second was a fey secretive dipsomaniac; the third had trouble with her back, a skin disease and false teeth with a built-in click – she could not bend to make a bed, she would neither wash up nor wash, and conversation with her was like talking to a representative of some African tribe.

My mother entertained and waited on this weird trio, hired to wait on her. She was more amused by their peculiarities than we were by their exorbitant fees. But she promised us that notwithstanding her infirmities she would do better without such broken reeds to lean on.

From then on she was looked after by a team of local part-timers, and as ever by Mrs Gulwell. She grew fond of Jean Jenkins, who lived over the stables and nursed her through innumerable crises, and Kathy Friend and Kathy Langley who took it in turns to spend the nights on call at Lyegrove – and again I would say the fondness was mutual. The latter pair were impressed by the courage of the two old ladies, Mama and Mrs Gulwell, whose custom it was to sleep at opposite ends of the alarmingly large and isolated house.

These arrangements were far from ideal in the opinion of Mama's children. A hundred and one eventualities might leave her stricken and unassisted. Mrs Gulwell was no longer capable of carrying a tray up the stairs to her – and vice versa for that matter. If one of the Kathys failed to clock in of an evening, because a car was faulty or snow blocked the road, she would be stuck in her chair in the front hall for the night. If Keith Hunter were to feel poorly and not like working, the electricity supply could go wrong – and nobody else seemed to be able to put it right – and the shopping for food in Chipping Sodbury would not get done.

The possibilities of emergencies so dire as to pose threats to existence itself were uncountable; and the only corrective action that could be taken in each case was for one of us to cancel all commitments and rush to the rescue. Agreement with the principle that she should live dangerously did not altogether dispel our concern for her welfare. On the other hand the threat of having to resign our responsibilities in order to assume full responsibility for hers led us to discuss alternatives. Was it really too late to move her into a smaller sensible house? Might she not be more comfortable and less lonely in the right institution?

She volunteered answers to these questions which none of us had liked to ask. She was awfully sorry to be such a nuisance. She supposed the unselfish thing for her to do would be to go into a home for old people. She just could not face it. She was really not unhappy as and where she was, pegging along in her usual way, and would be happier still if she were able to feel less of a burden. She begged us not to bother about her. She hoped and prayed her financial resources were and would be sufficient to cover her expenses. But of course she would leave Lyegrove if she absolutely had to and even if it broke her heart.

Not least amongst the faculties she retained was that of ruling the roost. In other words she continued to do as she pleased, which after all was most pleasing to us.

Besides, we were influenced by her pet proverb: the devil you know is better than the unknown one. Our reluctance to have our lives interrupted and interfered with seriously, however ready we were to lend her a hand now and then, denied us the right to interfere with her life. We could not and would not uproot her from where she said she was quite happy in order to plant her in some spot suitable by our standards, where she might be sad.

Her regular attendants, in a position to gauge the extent of her strength and weakness, with whom she had formed those inter-dependent relationships she always preferred to the merely social sort, settled it by speaking up in favour of the status quo.

MEMBERS OF THE opposite sex kept on adding bright touches of colour to her existence. Her dog Sing slept on her lap in the evenings. She had abbreviated the phrase she used for summoning Sing, which in its shorter form startled the uninitiated. Partly for a joke, instead of calling 'Come to Mother,' she now called the one word 'Mother!' – in response to which she would with luck be joined by a panting and pop-eyed male pekinese.

Another verbal pleasantry related to her rest in the afternoon. On working weekdays the drill was that her present gardener Keith Hunter would assist her from her upright chair into the armchair by the Pither stove and arrange her stool, rug, radio and so on. She was inclined to ask visitors after lunch to give Keith the message that she was ready to be put down.

Red letter days were those on which James Lees-Milne walked over from his house at Badminton to have tea with her, or she managed a meeting with Billy Henderson. She had first met Billy when he was commissioned to paint the picture of her in her sitting-room in her eighty-sixth year. Both friendships were on the passionate side, if as dignified as befitted the seniority and eminence of the parties concerned. My mother's romantic inclinations remind me of Fanny Burney's confidante Mrs Delany: a young woman asked Mrs Delany, who was then in her eighties, if it were not a relief to have outgrown and to be free of the pains of love, and received a reply to this effect: 'You'll have to put that question to someone older than me.'

Love of what could be called a more sacred kind, although there was no profanity in her associations with Jim and Billy, came her way in the form of a medal for services to the Roman Catholic Church awarded by the Pope.

She was an exemplary Catholic, I would suggest. Her piety had no tinge of the bigotry or even the excessive enthusiasm of the majority of converts, and she was prepared to ignore the more esoteric instructions of the authorities in the interests of common sense. Her firm faith must have helped her as she approached her Maker and to keep Rose's problems in perspective.

But it was not only for being good in a religious sense

that she got her medal. Annually for fifty-odd years she had organised a bring-and-buy sale on behalf of the Catholic Church in Chipping Sodbury: it took place at Lyegrove on the day she opened the house and garden to the public. Her fund-raising efforts were not confined to providing the premises where others would do the work. She slaved away month in and month out, making saleable objects while she was able to, extorting contributions from shops, collecting stock for her second-hand counter, and foisting raffle tickets on all and sundry. She was said to have been the main financial prop of local Catholicism; and the present priest and his congregation had banded together to sue for and obtain recognition for their bene-factress.

The presentation by a Bishop representing the Pope packed the Church Hall with my mother's co-religionists and friends. The family contingent was June, who had been brought up as the Catholic her French father would have wished her to be, and my brother, Rose and myself, permitted as children to follow in our Protestant father's footsteps. Strictly speaking, no doubt, Mama should have insisted on our practice of her religion – she may have broken solemn vows in order not to fuss her husband and their offspring with un-ecumenical shibboleths. Perhaps the divine right of Listers had entered into her decision to respect others' freedom of worship.

But when we three Protestants introduced ourselves as the skeletons in her cupboard, her guilty secret and badge of shame in triplicate, nobody pointed an accusing finger or seemed to want to strip her of the insignia of Papal approval.

This happy occasion gave rise to an example of Mrs Gulwell's wit which we all laughed at and loved her for. Soon after the investiture of Mama the Pope in person paid a visit to Britain. Mrs Gulwell commented: 'I expect we'll be having the old bugger to tea.'

Mrs Gulwell was a walking compendium of humanity with its sterling qualities and contradictions. She was fond of animals and throughout one spring and summer fed a vixen and the cubs it had given birth to – they lived in a disused woodshed some fifty yards from the kitchen windows. She would watch the cubs' shadowy games in the gloaming, and took a personal pride in their growth. But with the autumn came the Beaufort Hunt in charge of the old Duke of Beaufort, to whom Mrs Gulwell was heard to shout: 'They're over there, Your Grace!' My mother remonstrated as follows: 'How could you feed your foxes and look after them and then point out their hiding-place to the master of a pack of bloodthirsty hounds?' Mrs Gulwell replied: 'Well – I do like a bit of hunting.'

ESPECIALLY IN OLD age a birthday that marks the passing of ten years is much more of a rubicon than the nine birthdays in between.

I think it came as a nasty shock to my mother, realising she was about to be ninety and then in her ninety-first year. She owed her perennial youthfulness to planning fun for the future: by not looking back at the vista of the past she had been able to forget how long it was becoming. A part of her charm was still the element of giddy girl in her personality. But how could she be giddily girlish now she really was a nonagenarian and incapable of walking upstairs? How was she to flirt with men when she could scarcely see them or hear what they were saying? She had never pretended to be younger than she was; but suddenly there was no getting away from the fact that she was ancient.

My brother and sister-in-law gave a birthday party in her honour. She cavilled at the prospective celebration of so regrettable an anniversary. But she could not help looking forward to it in her eager sporting way, and took the unusually spendthrift step of buying herself a new dress in Chipping Sodbury.

And of course she enjoyed every minute of being as it were the belle of the ball again, and the centre of attention and on the receiving end of compliments and declarations of affection; and discussed the party in detail for weeks afterwards.

Perhaps at last the idea that she merited some congratulations slipped through the barrier of her modesty, and she too recognised the achievements of being loved by so many outsiders as well as her descendants, of the esteem in which she was generally held on account of her accomplishments, and of her durability. I hope she was at least momentarily pleased to have passed all the tests set by time and fate.

For under the influence of her access or excess of confidence she decided to disregard the advice of experts and well-wishers and go ahead with a surgical operation for the removal of a cataract on one of her eyes. She had been warned that performed on somebody of her age it was unlikely to be successful, and could make matters worse and affect the other eye. Besides the anaesthetic was dangerous. But she insisted. As for the danger, she was bound to discount it. She cited her age in support of the alternative argument that she did not have much life left to be spoiled by the failure of the operation. In her judgment the risk was worth taking for the potential reward of the restoration of her former clear-sightedness.

It went badly for her. The result of the surgery was that she could see considerably less well than she had before.

From one point of view even this cloud had a silver lining, although she was unaware of it and the rest of us had mixed feelings in respect of our awareness. The glory of her garden had departed. It was turning into a wilderness compared with what it used to be. But she was more or less blind to its shortcomings, and inclined to repeat her customary claim that it was better than ever.

Her estimate of its qualities may have been not merely a reflex action or wishful thinking, but based on her increasingly keen appreciation of the sights and scents that still got through to her. Her last love – so to speak – was to be pushed in her wheelchair round the garden and breathe the air and absorb the ambience fraught with memories of happiness.

The other side of the medal was that such jaunts made her fearful of losing her sight altogether. She was the more depressed because she felt she had been a fool to force the issue of the operation. Her spirit faltered before the spectres that seemed to encircle and crowd in on her: the relentless advance of Rose's illness, her own progressive debility, autumn coming with winter not far behind, and the realisation that also in a metaphorical sense the party was over. The new difficulties she had when it came to watching television tightened the occupational screw of old age – boredom. Even the prospect of next summer was spoilt by the thought that for her there might be no tennis from Wimbledon.

She told June, always her confidante, she was fed up and would not mind dying, an admission unique in the annals of her vitality – and distressing, however lightly she said it.

WE FINALLY PREVAILED on her to sleep downstairs in the sitting-room. We could no longer find people strong enough to carry her in her wheelchair up to bed. Tactfully or contrarily she loved it and wondered why she had not transplanted herself years ago. She was not too disapproving of our rearrangement of the furniture.

Gilly and I stayed at Lyegrove for the last weekend in November. Rose came to see us there, and we drove Mama over to see or anyway have a glass of sherry with David and Jane. As usual on the Sunday afternoon we were all sad to say goodbye: setting aside deep considerations of life and death, I once more felt torn between

[ 143 ]

helping her to eke out her existence and carrying on with my own.

A comforting reflection was that she would be joined by June on the following Friday – she only had the middle of the week to struggle through without a member of the family in attendance.

But on the Wednesday evening I was unable to speak to her on the telephone. She had had a bad night and been asleep for most of the day. I rang on Thursday. She said she was now all right, but for some reason had spent some twenty-four hours in a coma. I questioned her use of that alarming word and said I had been told she was simply sleeping.

Not a bit of it, she declared; she knew the difference between sleep and a coma perfectly well. And she described the extraordinary waking visions, not dreams, which had so amused her while she was semi-conscious. She had seen these little people – sweet midgets in evening dress – dancing on top of the tallboy opposite her bed.

I could not quite join in her laughter as she recalled her hallucinations. I had been worried before by her accounts of having seen the ghosts of relatives and friends.

Who were these midgets, were they recognisable, I asked.

No, she giggled at my stern tone, she had no idea who they were, she was not acquainted with many midgets, but they danced splendidly; and she issued a gentle challenge to my humourless anxiety by adding that she had reduced Rose to fits of laughter with her description of their antics.

When I rang up on the Friday evening June told me

[ 144 ]

she had put Mama to bed earlier than usual: she had been feeling groggy, had a cup of soup and a cigarette for supper, and then been pleased to settle down for the night.

The next morning June rang me to say she had died. Her bed-covers were not disarrayed: sleep must have borne her painlessly from this world into the next.

None of us could exactly regret the kindness of her death. Moreover she had lived the fullest life, and although she suffered many hard blows in her youth and middle age she had been born lucky, blessed with good health, beauty and brains, and had had more happiness than most people in the end.

Our sadness lay in knowing how much we were going to miss her.

Her funeral was to be at the Roman Catholic Church in Chipping Sodbury, and she would be buried with her Protestant husband – my father – in Little Badminton churchyard. Instructions were given to the undertakers to drive at a fair pace the seven miles from Chipping Sodbury to Little Badminton, so as not to prolong the mournful business unnecessarily. After the service the hearse with wreaths of flowers on its roof-rack drove off and was followed by the family in various cars. As the hearse gathered speed, and then passed the entrances to the front and back drives of Lyegrove, the flowers on top of it shook their heads in the breeze gallantly and gaily.

Those pretty innocent flowers, seeming to enjoy being blown about in the breeze, almost to be laughing at the fun of it and urging us to cheer up, were like my mother.

# Index

[ 146 ]